Gladys S[...]
2004.

Memoirs of Our Farming Days

Mary Rose Baker

ATHENA PRESS
LONDON

MEMOIRS OF OUR FARMING DAYS
Copyright © Mary Rose Baker 2004

ISBN 1 84401 252 2

First Published 2004 by
ATHENA PRESS
Queen's House, 2 Holly Road
Twickenham, TW1 4EG
United Kingdom

Printed for Athena Press

Memoirs of Our Farming Days

To Maggie, for all her encouragement and help.

Prologue

The long-awaited day had arrived at last; the day when we were to experience the most amazing change in our lifestyle. John and I had left behind our family and friends, good jobs and the comfort of a modern, centrally-heated bungalow. Now we were here, waving goodbye to the removers and feeling very alone in our run-down smallholding and farmhouse. Our daydreams had become reality, but suddenly the enormity of what we had done was scary: we had no positive plans and very little money behind us. John, as usual, was unfazed and optimistic, but I was haunted by people's attitudes. Hetty had said we were fools, Uncle Ken said, 'You'll starve', others said, 'Whatever made you decide to do this?'

Well, it all began with those glorious days spent at Uncle Ken's farm on Exmoor…

When he suggested we spend a week in his caravan we happily agreed. His camping field was in an idyllic spot, overlooked by a bluebell wood with a river bubbling alongside, deer grazing on the distant hills and rabbits scurrying here and there. We couldn't wait to get down there again. Unfortunately his caravan was booked for the rest of the summer, so we decided to buy one ourselves. We found a small touring caravan, which we towed down with our Morris 1000, and Uncle Ken persuaded us to leave it in his field permanently so that we could go there for weekends and holidays. Consequently, for three happy years we experienced the beauty of Exmoor and the workings of a farm.

John learnt to use Uncle's shotgun and he went shooting rabbits. I didn't like the idea of this at first, but it was part of the country scene and rabbits were a nuisance in the fields. After eating the first one, cooked over our campfire, I was won over and often accompanied John in his search for more.

One day there was a clay pigeon shoot on the moors, and Uncle insisted that John had a go. He was delighted when his 'pupil' managed to shoot down two clays.

We decided to try fishing, as all the other campers seemed to go down and catch little trout from the river, but for some reason we weren't lucky with that. In fact, it was an hilarious experience. The first fish we caught was a dead one which we landed on the little beach, and then when John was casting his line again it caught on the branch of a tree and took us ages to recover. Another time he slipped into the river and emerged soaking wet. So all things considered we decided to give up fishing, which was just as well because we forgot to lock our fishing tackle in the caravan one weekend and when we returned the following weekend it had disappeared. We weren't really sorry.

It was in the spring of 1968 that we first started camping, and in October our daughter, Maggie, married Iain, and shortly afterwards they moved into their own house.

Later that year Aunty Dolly was waiting for us when we arrived at the farm. She said, 'Do look in the hedge by the caravan – there's a cat down there with two new kittens. Keep an eye on her and see that she's all right.'

The cat had come from a nearby farm, but the people had moved away and left her behind. We found that the campers were feeding her quite adequately and all three looked well. One kitten was really beautiful, a very pale ginger – almost pink underneath – and walking proudly behind his mother with his tail in the air. We fell in love with him and took him home with us. We called him Shandy, and Maggie was able to look after him when we were away.

We did plenty of jobs on the farm in lieu of paying 'rent' for the caravan pitch. We kept the hedges tidy on the long lane to the road; we helped in the garden; we plucked many chickens and ducks, and we helped Uncle move stock around. It all made us more determined to find a place of our own, as we wanted to spend all our time in the country.

We liked to cross the stepping-stones and walk along the river bank to Tarr Steps, a renowned beauty spot. Sometimes Aunt and Uncle would suggest taking us for a walk and showing us new places. One Sunday we went to South Batsom a short distance away where they had more land. It was so quiet and peaceful there, the only sound being the occasional cry of a bird of prey as it hopefully swooped for food – buzzards were commonplace there.

Our other favourite was a walk through Hayes Wood, especially at bluebell time when there was a blanket of blue between the trees, dazzling whenever the sun shone through. Once we were startled by rustling above us and saw several red deer chasing one another, so close to us – an exciting experience.

In May 1970 Michael was born. A year later Maggie and Iain, having purchased a large tent, brought him to the farm. Uncle Ken made such a fuss of him. He and Aunty Dolly hadn't any children, but he loved them – especially boys. Michael was so interested in everything.

We had already started to enquire about small properties on Exmoor. We looked at the strangest places, but anything worthwhile was out of our price range. Uncle was not at all enthusiastic or helpful. One day, when he and I were alone, he suggested knocking down the two pigsties that he was so proud of having built himself but were no longer used. He said we could have a decent mobile home in their place. It was adjacent to his house and would have a lovely view of the river. He had even worked out how we could make an adequate income there. I realised that he didn't want to lose us, but I knew it was not what we wanted, so I pretended not to take him seriously. John agreed when I told him later.

We now decided to find something the other side of South Molton: outside of, but not far from, Exmoor. We found Kinnings for sale in Chittlehamholt. We walked down the very steep, stony lane to the house. The owner, who had been widowed the previous year, was no longer living in the house, but was there to show us around.

The ceilings were so low that John had to stoop to get into the kitchen. In the top room there was a stuffed bird in a glass case, and the mirrors all had cloths covering them because the lady was afraid of lightning. It all seemed very strange to us, and the house having been unoccupied for some months didn't help. There were two front doors to the house, one leading into the lower room and kitchen and the other into the top room. I was about to open the second door when she almost shrieked, 'Don't open that door! Us never opens that door!' I was quite nervous, wondering what was wrong, and was anxious to get away.

As we were leaving John started asking about the rates and so on. Once we were out of hearing I said, 'Why on earth were you asking that? Nothing would make me live in that house – I could never live there!'

We looked around outside. There were only fourteen acres left – the rest having already been sold – but there were four good fields and a nice shippen with tie-up for eight cows and dairy attached. There were several outbuildings; all needing much attention, but it was the best we had found at an affordable price.

John was quite keen, so I gave in, rang the agent and agreed on the asking price of £7,500. We then sold our bungalow, the caravan, our 3.4 Jaguar, a piano, sets of books and other items until we could manage to purchase Kinnings without a mortgage. When people asked why we did it, we tried to explain it was a dream coming true.

So, we're back to the beginning of the story when we first moved in…

Chapter I

1971

It was a fine autumn day when we moved, rather cloudy at first, but when we arrived at our new home the sun greeted us, and it was quite a lot warmer than when we had travelled through the mists of the Brendon hills and Exmoor. The house seemed very strange to us, seen for the first time empty. It was in a state of disrepair, and we realised that there would be hard work ahead. Shandy had to be shut safely in the shippen with his litter box, food and drink. He sounded very unhappy, but I felt sure he would enjoy this life as much as we would when he recovered from the initial shock.

The removers found their way with only one wrong turning, though they were rather daunted by the narrow Devon lanes with their high hedges on either side. We said, 'Just put the things anywhere,' and so they did! Heaven only knows when we shall get straight!

No fitted kitchens here, and the ceiling in the kitchen seems lower than ever. All the men had to stoop to avoid knocking their heads! I'm glad I'm only 5 ft 6 in., but even I kept bending just in case.

The noise of the automatic pump, which fills our water tank from the well, startled us all at first, but we shall soon get used to it. Poor Shandy jumped with fright and started crawling about on his stomach. He is enjoying the fields, though, and next morning we discovered a mouse neatly laid out for inspection. It was to be the first of many.

We lit the Rayburn upon our arrival and were pleased to see how quickly it heated the water so we were able to have hot baths after our long, exhausting day. We had no curtains ready for the windows, but it didn't really matter since the house isn't overlooked by anybody. We lay in bed and watched the clouds chasing each other across the moon and made our plans for the next day.

We spent the next morning unpacking. After an early dinner we drove to Barnstaple – a journey of about thirteen miles – and it was raining when we arrived. We found the shops most interesting, particularly those on Butcher's Row, which consists of several butcher's shops all displaying fresh and appetising meat. Such competition!

After tea we walked around our bottom field to pick blackberries, but unfortunately they were mostly overripe. Our neighbours from the next farm came and introduced themselves: Rosalyn and Sam Wright and their two small children, Christopher, fifteen months, and Samantha, two and a half years. They lived in the farmhouse and his parents in the chalet, which was only one field away from us. Sam was asking for grass keep, and he agreed to enquire about prices for keep at the market the following day and contact us again. They seemed very friendly, and his family had lived in the house for forty-three years.

On the third day we set about cleaning and decorating. The weather was good so we started outside, painting the doors and gate black. The walls were to be painted white later. We fixed a cat-flap for Shandy, although he protested about it as it wasn't the same type as his previous one. He turned up while I was meeting our post woman for the first time, his ginger face blackened with soot and cobwebs! He had obviously found his way up the chimney, and this pointed us to yet another job: two chimneys to be cleaned. The second one was choked up with sticks, and we decided the birds must have been nesting in it.

The post woman informed us that she was married to a farmer and just did her job for pin money. She's a very pleasant person, and there is a right of way for her across our fields to get to the next farm.

This had been a very hot day – the temperature in our bedroom was 70°F – and we both spent a rather restless night, due partly to heat and partly to excitement and overtiredness.

Rosalyn surprised us by saying she only used wood on her Rayburn – except at Christmas time when she bought a little solid fuel when visitors were coming – as she found it easier to regulate the cooking with this. We had brought two bags of coal with us, but immediately tried wood only, and were delighted with it and the amount of really hot water it provided, as well as with the money we saved, as we could collect all the wood from around the farm. With our own water supply and the rates at an unbelievable £16 a year, we felt we should be able to manage. We aimed to keep a few cows and hens, do bed and breakfast and possibly buy a caravan to let.

Our first Sunday started bright, and John commenced to Snowcem the outside walls, while I coped with the full Sunday dinner in the Rayburn. The worst part about it was spending so much time looking for the various utensils, many of which were still packed. I cooked pork, stuffing, applesauce, roast and boiled potatoes and cabbage, followed by blackberries and apples and custard, as well as a batch of raspberry buns. It all tasted delicious.

I felt quite exhausted by dinnertime, but very pleased with myself.

The rain started in the afternoon, heavy clouds loomed suddenly overhead and down it came, continuing for most of the day. We noticed the rain came under both of our front doors.

John and I made a start on decorating the dining room, the walls in pale green emulsion, and ceiling and paintwork in brilliant white. We would have liked to have spent a longer time stripping off all the old paper first, but it might have proved to be a long and difficult job, and we had so many other jobs requiring attention.

Monday was dry again, but misty over the hills, and John decided it was not suitable to work outside so he continued in the dining room while I did the washing. The automatic pump worked overtime, as my washing machine takes a great quantity of water for rinsing. I used the lines which had been left in the field, but they weren't really satisfactory. First John had to clear a way for me to go through the little gate from the garden. Five thick posts stood in the field with galvanised wire strung between them – enough room for a month's washing to dry! There was only one prop, so all the longest things had to hang together and be propped up or else they dangled in the grass.

'Never mind,' said John, 'you've always said you'd like a field to hang your washing in!'

It's quite true that it caught the little wind that was blowing and dried quite quickly so that I was able to iron the lot during the afternoon. It smelt so fresh and sweet.

John went into Barnstaple in the afternoon to report to the employment exchange. He wanted to get a temporary job until the spring. The clerk thumbed through a few cards and shook his head. 'You blokes certainly pose us a problem,' he sighed. 'There's a job here in the civil service, but if I sent you they'd send you straight back to me.'

John was rather relieved, actually, as there was so much to be done at the house.

Sam and his father came over during the evening. They suggested putting bullocks in three of our fields to get the grass down and finishing up with sheep until the end of the year. For this we would be paid £25. It suited us as the grass was going to waste. They said that Well Field had a reputation for the best grass in the area. Their dog drank Shandy's cream, and we picked blackberries in Hill Field – beauties! We also discovered sloes and more hazelnuts. John said there was a holly tree in berry in the orchard. Fresh discoveries every day!

The Tuesday was a perfect day again – cloudless blue sky and warm. John was busy with Snowcem all day. I weeded the rockery and washed all the upstairs floors with Handy Andy. The Wrights repaired gaps in the hedges, and by the evening they had thirty-five bullocks in Well Field. They looked beautiful in the lush green grass, particularly the Devon rubies with their deep red, velvety coats. In the evening we cleaned the dining room floor in readiness for the carpet being fitted the next day and John tidied the implement shed. I lettered a board 'KINNINGS' ready to fix to the stone pillar at the entrance.

On Wednesday John finished his first coat of Snowcem on the two visible walls. The rest would have to wait for the time being. He was up early with the gun, but there was no sign of a rabbit, although we could see their holes in the banks and their runs through the grass. Actually, it was misty and very cold first thing after a slight ground frost, so I expect they were staying in their warm burrows.

The sun was out brilliantly again after nine o'clock and it started to warm up. We spent most of the afternoon laying carpet in the dining room. Of course, the door of the cupboard under the stairs wouldn't go over it, and John couldn't get the door off – double hinges top and bottom and countless screws all nicely painted in. He finally managed to saw enough off to get the door fixed. It was all worth it when the furniture was in position and polished with our lovely pink vases washed and in their places. John's barometer (a present from his firm) was in pride of place on the wall. I made the curtains in the evening and we hung those, but the nails, which John had carefully removed, had to go back to take the curtain wire – three-inch nails of all things, as the little hooks just wouldn't hold. Our removal man had said you could see it was people of low standards living here before, but it seems they had no alternative…

We had great trouble with swarms of flies in the two end bedrooms. They came in through the light fittings in their dozens, evidently from the loft. We killed off hundreds of them, and John sprayed the loft where they were obviously breeding.

We had now been in our new house for a week, and with the one room furnished to our satisfaction we felt very happy.

I made up more curtains, but had nothing but trouble with them – even three-inch nails just disappeared into the cob. The house itself was of the queerest construction – especially under the floorboards, where the ceiling seemed to be made from a kind of slate. We managed to get a bedroom ready for Maggie and Iain, but it wasn't very nice yet; it badly needed redecorating. Of course the door wouldn't go over the carpet again. I suppose it was all very amusing really, but we were too tired to appreciate it just then.

We were getting excited about our family's first visit. They were due to arrive on the Friday evening. That morning we went to South Molton shopping in readiness for them, and were delighted to bump into Uncle and Aunty. We sat in the back of their car for a long chat. They said there was a rumour going around the village that we had been left some money. We'd also heard another rumour suggesting we had moved to Kinnings to grow grapes – both quite ridiculous notions, of course!

Maggie, Iain and Michael arrived at twenty past seven, all rather tired after their tedious eighty-mile journey – the motorway had not yet been built. Little Michael soon recovered when he saw his granddad.

We had supper in the dining room, the first time we had used the big table. I hoped it would be fine the following day so that they could enjoy some fresh air at Kinnings and look around – it was too dark that night. Yes, Saturday was a fine day, so we all walked around the fields and studied the views.

Below Meadow Field stood the tall conifers. One day they would have to be cut down for timber and fresh ones planted in their place, but not just yet we hoped. From Well Field we looked down towards the river, the railway line and the main road to Barnstaple. Beyond that the land rose sharply and we could see a few scattered farms in the distance. Our lane up to the road was steep and stony – not easy to walk on. The road itself was narrow, allowing only single traffic. In places there was grass growing in the middle, which caused great amusement to some of our visitors.

When the viewing was over, Iain and John set to work on the tractor. We had taken over an ancient one, which started on petrol and then ran on TVO. We hoped it would do until we could afford something better. They spent many hours on this, both Saturday and Sunday. Anyway, they made it move around the field, so that was progress, but it would still need more attention on their next visit...

When they went home on Sunday afternoon, Kinnings seemed so quiet without them and I felt quite sad for a time. John said, 'This is because they aren't just two miles away anymore,' and whisked me off blackberrying again in Top Field where the lovely view cheered me up somewhat.

After tea we spent an hour sorting out the rubbish tip the previous people had left behind, as the dustcart was due on Tuesday. There was only a fortnightly collection. Rosalyn didn't know which day, as she didn't put anything out for them and it seems that our predecessors didn't either! Goodness knows what they did with their rubbish – just left it buried somewhere in the garden, we think.

I now had a clothesline up in the garden, which was much better – especially as the bullocks were in Clothesline Field. They pushed the garden gate open that evening and John had to get a few of them back into the field.

Now that we had finished all we wanted to in the house for the time being we had to get busy again on the outhouses. John started on the portable fowl house, for which we had to pay £2. He practically had to remake the thing, but we thought it would be useable eventually as we only intended to start off with a few free-range birds for ourselves. John also started cleaning out the shippen in readiness for Clara's arrival. I had decided a long time ago that our first cow would be called Clara. Actually, I have always been terrified of cows, but giving one a name seemed to make it less frightening.

We were relieved on Tuesday to see that the dustmen had removed two bags of rubbish as well as emptying our bin, but it was going to take months to get rid of the lot.

Rosalyn rang inviting me to tea the next day, which I accepted. We had a very pleasant afternoon, but her children were a real handful. When I left she gave me apples to take home, including Cornish gillyflowers. They were absolutely beautiful. I'd never heard of them before, and the flavour was wonderful. We were also introduced to Mrs Wright senior, who immediately invited John and me around on Friday evening at about seven o'clock. There was more social life here than where we came from!

On Friday evening we walked across Well Field to the chalet. It was very dark and raining, but we had a small torch. Suddenly we were confronted by the bullocks, who had decided to investigate us. They came so close that I was really scared and shook with fright until we reached the gate and safety.

We spent a pleasant evening with Mr and Mrs Wright. They were very hospitable and provided supper and lots of information about local matters and about their family. We left them at about eleven o'clock, and as we were leaving John mentioned the bullocks in the field so Mr Wright insisted on seeing us home. He had a good lamp, but there wasn't a single bullock in the lower field. Typical!

Now the visits were over for the time being we went

to work again, mostly out of doors. John moved all of last year's hay to one end of the barn in readiness for getting the new in. He saw a rat and discovered a nest there. 'Ah! Just the cat I want – I've got a job for you,' he said when he spied Shandy helping me hang out the washing, but Shandy wasn't too keen on rats and was rather indignant when taken forcibly to the spot. He just sat there washing himself for a few seconds and then scampered off. However, he's still catching mice, and if you lift him up he belches. It serves him right.

By mid-October we were experiencing terrific gales and rain, and we heard of flooding in other parts of the country, including Bristol. We thought that perhaps the hills would save us, but within an hour the heavens had opened on us as well. John made an inspection of his new ditching and was pleased with his diversion, but he had reckoned without floodwater. As the rain became more torrential and prolonged, the gullies became quite inadequate and the streams of muddy water poured straight into the shippen and dairy which we had been working so hard to clean out. Rain also gushed under and through the front door of the house.

When I could find any spare time I wrote to friends and family, and we loved receiving their letters in return, especially acceptances to our invitations. It kept the post woman quite busy. A correspondence from the post office amused us greatly. It informed us that they would pay us 10 p per annum for keeping two of their poles on our land!

Then we received the deeds from the solicitor, but there was no indication of the age of Kinnings. The first date mentioned in abstract title was 1811, but we learned later that it was built in the sixteenth century.

Apart from family, our first visitors were Margaret and Dorothy from Portishead in Somerset. They spent a Sunday with us. It was a fine day, mainly sunny and warm, which was perfect for our walk around the 'estate', admiring the views from the top field. They were quite taken with the house. The dining room really did look attractive by now, but other parts had all the character of an old cob building! The low, uneven ceiling in the kitchen was no trouble to people less than 5 ft 8 in., so that was all right for this visit! John had noticed, however, that he could stand quite comfortably at the sink, so he had no excuse for getting out of the washing up!

Our visitors left soon after tea and we returned to our work in the orchard. We lit a bonfire, which crackled away merrily throughout the evening.

The next day our first livestock arrived: six four-month-old pullets from Sam. We soon had them shut up in their refurbished house, which Rosalyn called a first-class hotel. After dinner we set off to buy some corn and chicken wire to make them a run. Later we had a phone call to say that a dozen pullets we had ordered from Tedburn St Mary would be arriving in two days' time.

Next day when John let the six birds out Shandy's face was an absolute picture – he'd never seen poultry before, and he watched in amazement as they walked away towards the shippen. He stood there uncertain whether to give chase or run away and looked to me for guidance. I explained that they were ours and not to be chased, which he seemed to understand, as he took little further interest in them.

John's father was our next visitor. He came by train from Bristol to Exeter and John picked him up from there. It was good to see him again, especially as he was one of the few people who really approved of our venture. He was fascinated with Kinnings, but after a quick look around we insisted that he had a good rest after his journey; he has angina so must take care. We spent a lovely evening chatting and exchanging news.

The next day I rang Uncle Ken to say his brother Dick was staying with us, so he and Aunty arrived to see him in the afternoon. At the same time twelve golden comets were delivered and had to be housed in the loft of the implement shed, so it was all quite hectic. At least it showed Uncle we were making a start!

Dad stayed with us for a week and was a great help. He enjoyed stoking up the bonfire and getting rid of rubbish, even using the reap hook. He helped me creosote a gate while John started the second coat of Snowcem on the house. He also managed to get up our steep, rough lane to the 'main road' (as he jokingly called it), making use of a makeshift seat halfway that John had fixed for him. He assured us when he left that the exercise had been good for his heart, and he felt better than he had done for a long time. We are all looking forward to his visit next year. He insisted on lending us money to buy cows, and with John just having received his first unemployment benefit and some income tax rebate, we were now able to go ahead with more plans.

After Dad left the family arrived and Maggie and Michael were staying for the whole week. Our man looked a real little farmer in his welly boots, following Granddad everywhere and helping to feed the birds.

One afternoon an electrician came to fix more points and do the wiring for an immersion heater, followed later by the plumber to fit the heater. The plumber was a very friendly man and most interested in what we were doing. He assured us that he would always be available in an emergency – even on a Sunday or Bank Holiday, and this turned out to be the case. Then a lady from the village came with poppies. We shall never be lonely here!

The same afternoon, Rosalyn brought Samantha and Christopher over. What a hectic time! Christopher ate some red berries from the cotoneaster bush; Samantha weed on the garden path, and both boys had good bangs on the head, with subsequent screaming. Then Michael helped himself to a packet of cigarettes from the electrician's pocket, which I replaced quickly and hoped they weren't too squashed, and Samantha went home with Maggie's watch on her wrist. This was only discovered later!

On the Sunday John finished the second coat of Snowcem and the improvement was amazing. Kinnings was really beginning to look smart. With creosote on the field gates and outbuildings, Presomet covering the rusty roofs, brambles dug out from behind the house and weeds removed and burnt from the garden and orchard it was a transformation.

We noticed a caravan advertised in *The Journal* for £87, as well as some Aylesbury ducklings and decided to go after these the next day. After dinner we all went to Ashreigney to collect twelve ducklings. John took a cardboard box with two-inch wire across the top, and when he carried them out to the car all their necks were poking up through the wire and they were making a fine old din. Didn't they stink the car out! Michael alone seemed oblivious of this and stood on the back seat leaning over the yellow creatures quite enraptured and constantly turning to inform us, most importantly, that they were chicken. 'Ducks,' we all replied.

'*Chicken*,' insisted Michael. Ah well, what's in a name?

We continued to Torrington with the ducklings – with all the car windows well opened – and bought a double bed. This was tied to the roof rack, and fortunately the rain held off for our return journey. The ducklings were put in a wired-off section of the loft and were very nervous at first. They kept rushing to the furthest corner when anyone approached, but finally they huddled down together and slept.

The next morning John and I went to Martinhoe Cross to see the caravan and thought it was a bargain at £87 – an old type, but aluminium and freshly painted inside and out, with new curtains and covers. It was sixteen feet long with an end kitchen. We hoped to let it during high season.

In the afternoon John went to Bow to collect three ducks and a drake. This time he went alone, but he assured us that they didn't smell half as bad as the ducklings. These four were to go into one of the piggeries for the time being. At last we were beginning to look more like a farm.

All the birds, including the ducks, followed John around all day – very comical. Later that day the caravan arrived, towed by a Humber Super Snipe (free delivery). We were really quite pleased with it, and thought it would be good for letting the next summer.

We were surprised when Rosalyn held a Tupperware party, and later on there was another one at the manor. These were good opportunities for me to meet more local people. I was regarded very much as a townie, but I no longer felt like one.

The evenings were getting cold and we decided to light a log fire in the dining room rather than sit in the kitchen by the Rayburn. We had a very large red brick fireplace needing huge logs, and the welcome warmth it gave out was most comforting after a busy day.

Rosalyn rang one morning to say her aunt and uncle at Meshaw had some laying hens for sale. As none of our young birds were due to lay yet, we decided to go to Meshaw and we came home with six nine-month-old pullets and six twenty-one-month-old hens. When John fed them next morning he picked up three eggs and a further four in the afternoon. It was so exciting to get our first eggs!

Unfortunately, the Rayburn, with which we had been so delighted, was now letting us down. It had been smoking a little depending on the wind direction, but had suddenly become so bad that we were suffocating. We were forced to open all the doors and windows and even to stand in the garden to breathe fresh air – not the best place on a cold November evening! It was even necessary to put the wretched thing out. Luckily we had just bought a Baby Belling as a standby for cooking. The recently fitted immersion heater gave us hot water and we had brought an electric convector heater with us, so we had a little warmth.

The next day we were off to Barnstaple to purchase an asbestos 'H' pipe to fix to the chimney, and this certainly helped. It was obvious, though, that the chimney needed sweeping. Unfortunately John was unable to open the plate on the flue pipe to get the brush up because the screws had seized up. It took a couple of days and lots of patience to remove the plate. The chimney was finally swept and all was well, just in time for me to make two Christmas cakes and two and a half dozen mince pies for the freezer.

The hens continued to lay on average five eggs a day,

and they now had the company of a maran cockerel, a handsome fellow named Charlie. He soon led them into bad ways, taking them into the garden and pecking at our sprouts and spring cabbage plants. Then they scratched in my rockeries and I really lost my temper with them. I flung some old green stuff out into the lane and they, together with the ducks, quickly demolished it. Charlie cockerel was always the ringleader, and what with his crowing at some unearthly hour long before dawn, I was fast going off him!

The weather at the end of November turned cold, wet and windy so we had to work inside. We tackled our top room at last, stripping off the faded wallpaper and knocking away the cracked plaster. John had to cement the wall in places and then re-plaster ready for papering. We used embossed wallpaper and painted it white, which together with an orange carpet, brought from the bungalow, and green and black furniture completely transformed the room.

Our greatest disappointment at this time was our inability to find any freshly calved Jersey heifers. Markets, farm sales and dealers had nothing to offer. We had thoroughly cleaned and disinfected the shippen and dairy and sterilised the milking equipment, which had also been serviced ready for use. We had registered as dairy farmers and had our water supply tested. We had hay and straw delivered and were just waiting impatiently for Clara and friend. We were getting short of money and had arranged an overdraft with the bank. John had been using the tractor quite a lot – thanks to Iain's hard work on it – but we would need a more modern one eventually, when we could afford it.

The television set that we had brought with us was useless here. We needed a new aerial, but the firm in

South Molton quoted twenty to thirty pounds including erection, and said it could be money wasted on our old set. We finally decided to rent one from them. It was essential that we had a television for when we were to take in paying guests next year.

On December 1st the men arrived with the television set and erected the aerial. It needed the addition of an amplifier, as our house was rather sheltered. I had just put their tea on a tray in the dining room when the rector, the Rev. Dampier-Bennett, called with the monthly newssheet and welcomed us to the village. Unfortunately he was in a hurry, but still managed to shake hands with me three times! His hands were so cold, but I imagine they had warmed up by the time he had walked back up our lane!

The family were with us from 14th to 19th December, but they wanted to be in their own home for Christmas. We expected to have a quiet time here, but were pleased to have a visit on the 21st from the dairy husbandry advisor. She was very optimistic about our venture, which cheered us up greatly.

That evening we were pleasantly surprised by the arrival of carol singers – at least fourteen of them – with lanterns and torches. They had walked across the field from Sam's and gathered outside our open door to sing. I was glad they could see into our bright cheery room. We had fixed fairy lights over the fireplace and had the log fire burning. With Christmas cards and letters arriving, visits from Sam, Rosalyn and Mr Wright, meeting with Ken and Dolly in South Molton and the bustle of shoppers in Barnstaple, we had no time to feel lonely.

On Christmas Eve Rosalyn turned up with some cream for us and I handed over the children's 'crackers'.

In the evening Mr Wright knocked at the door to wish us a merry Christmas, and then stayed chatting for nearly two hours. We were fortunate to have such good neighbours. We then went to midnight mass at Warkleigh church. It is an old church, situated in a farmyard and some distance from Warkleigh village. There was a congregation of just twenty-three, but the six carols sounded great with the support of a good organ. The rector recognised us and actually remembered our names. We liked him and were sorry he was due to retire.

Christmas day was dry and very mild, but we lit the log fire and opened our presents. A friend rang us in the morning and after dinner we rang Maggie. She had Grampy and my brother, Ted, there for the day, so we enjoyed chatting to all of them. We had a good walk afterwards and apart from feeding the birds did no work at all. We had one unexpected visitor – a little mouse that scampered across the kitchen floor, disappeared, and was never seen again. I expect he met up with Shandy.

On the last day of the year we drove Sam to Barnstaple. No luck with cows in the market, but we were pleased to be introduced to our other neighbour, David Harris of Presbury. He shook hands and seemed very friendly. Little did we know then that we were to enjoy a long, lasting friendship with him, even after leaving Kinnings...

In the afternoon we took half a dozen eggs to Mr and Mrs Wright and half a dozen to Rosalyn and collected from Ros a bantam and four chicks.

Chapter II
1972

A new year had started, and what would it have in store for us? We were advertising in the London *Evening Standard* for bed, breakfast and evening meal, as the house was just about ready. We were almost ready for cows, only waiting for Gascoigne's service engineer to check the milking equipment. He turned up at last on the 5th to change rubbers and with a new pulsator. Unfortunately his van stuck in mud outside the shippen and John had to get him out with the tractor, then his starter motor failed so John had to tow him up to the road!

On January 8th we went to Taunton market and were excited to see a number of freshly calved Jersey heifers. We were unused to buying at auction, but John managed to get three for £234. We arranged transport for them and they arrived at Kinnings just after six o'clock. On the way home we decided on names for them and the best one – of course – would be Clara. 'How about choosing names alphabetically?' I suggested, and we decided on Annabel for one. The third one had little horns and had been very frisky in the market, and we finally agreed that the name Betsy would suit her.

Mr Wright and Sam came straight over to help tie them up in the shippen, and later on Sam and Rosalyn came across and Rosalyn helped John to clean one of the clusters ready for milking in the morning. She knew a little about this as she came from a dairy farming family. The next morning she came across to help John with the milking, accompanied by Sam, Christopher, Samantha and Mr Wright! Despite the audience, the cows managed to produce four gallons of milk.

As it was mild and sunny we let the cows out in Lane Field and they immediately went up to the top, out of sight, and stayed there all day. We went up to inspect them at times and they seemed quite happy, but when Sam came over at four o'clock to help John get them in, he noticed that Clara wasn't well. Mr Wright advised us to get the vet, who arrived within the hour. He said Clara had a chill and high temperature, probably from the market. He gave her an injection and told John to make her a sacking coat. John and I went down alone to try milking, but couldn't manage the machine. Sam's brother-in-law, Owen, who was visiting them came after chapel and milked them for us. He was very pleasant and helpful.

Next day John was up early for milking and he managed fairly well – thanks to Owen's instructions. We had to throw Clara's milk away because she was ill. The vet came again and said she still had a temperature. A dreadful afternoon followed! Mr Wright came across at about half past two to put Annabel and Betsy in the shippen because of the start of heavy rain, but they escaped behind the shippen, jumped over the brambles into Meadow, charged down to the woods and into neighbouring fields. Annabel was captured soon after four o'clock, but Betsy was only lured back in the dark at half past five with an escort of young bullocks and the assistance of Sam's dog Carlo! Everybody was exhausted, and there was still the milking to do. It was quite a job coping with the milk until it was collected for the dairy. At nine o'clock I scalded some in one of our big cream pans. The book said it would reach the correct scalding time in thirty-five to fifty minutes, but the Rayburn had cooled down and it took hours. I got to bed at quarter to one!

Betsy continued to be frisky, and all this fuss did not help Clara. The vet came every day for a week, giving her more injections and ordering drenches and finally bringing his boss for a second opinion. He said her stomach was out of order, her lungs badly scarred, her heart weakening and one lung was rapidly filling up with fluid. So this was the end. We rang Tellam's, the knacker's yard, to come and take her. Mr Wright kindly took her to his farm and promised they would use a humane killer on the spot. I was at the kitchen sink when I saw her through the window, still in her sacking coat, walking slowly past in the pouring rain. I just broke down and cried and cried.

We had kept the dealer informed of her illness, and now I had to let him know the bad news. He was very sympathetic – especially knowing our circumstances – and asked us to let him know the vet's charge. Later we were relieved to receive a cheque from him covering half the cost of Clara and half the cost of veterinary treatment, which was really very generous of him.

These days were eventful in other ways, too. Our certificate of registration as dairy farmers had arrived. We had our first booking for the house – for the spring Bank Holiday week – and an enquiry from a nurse at Guy's hospital for two weeks in February. We started having power cuts as the miners are striking for more money. This interfered with our milking times and affected our water supply when the electric pump stopped bringing our water from the well.

We met someone in the market who had Ayrshire cows for sale at Berrynarbor, and we decided to go and see them. We had decided that we needed eight cows in the shippen to get a decent monthly milk cheque.

The ducklings had reached the right age to be killed, so John had this unpleasant job, and then we both plucked them. There were feathers all over the kitchen and all over us. It was a horrible performance, but something we would have to get used to.

The good news was that this same week I sold five-dozen eggs, and we had just picked up our first duck egg. I had made our first butter successfully – although it was an arm-aching job with a hand churn! This and the clotted cream were daily chores now, but we were selling quite a lot, eating quite a lot and putting the surplus in the freezer. One day, in addition to butter and cream, I made three batches of scones, a gooseberry pie and three apple tarts. Sam brought us a big bag of apples before Christmas, which were keeping well. Another day I made nineteen pounds of marmalade from Seville oranges. It only cost 41/2 p per pound. I also made lemon curd.

John was also kept busy outside. He started digging in the top garden. It was very wet and sticky, but it had to be done while time and weather allowed. Another day he went on a local fox shoot with neighbouring farmers and they shot two foxes. The sheep farmers were anxious about their lambs, and one had lost poultry to a fox recently.

John had also started cleaning up the old shippen – which had not been used for years – and I helped him with this. We went to Berrynarbor to inspect the Ayrshire cows and chose three that we could afford. A fifth calver, Emma, for £120, a sixth calver, Felicity, for £110 and a heifer, Caroline, for £130 were to be delivered on 10th February.

On the day they arrived we had sad news from Aunty Edie that Bob, her husband, had died. Edie was a cousin of John's father. She was eighty years old, a true countrywoman and most interested in our new life style. We felt obliged to go to the funeral, near Weymouth, as they had both been so kind to us in the past. We managed it thanks to Mr Wright keeping an eye on the farm for us and tying the cows in the shippen ready for the afternoon milking.

February 10th was a very busy day altogether, aside from the three cows arriving and the news of Uncle Bob. While I was on the phone there was a loud bang on the window, and on going outside to investigate I discovered a beautiful cock pheasant on the grass, still warm but quite dead. The poor bird had flown against the window and killed itself! Never mind, it would make a nice meal for the nurse!

After dinner two tons of hay arrived, which John had to carry bale by bale to the hay barn as there was no way through for a vehicle.

Next day John was up at five o'clock to beat the power cuts, which had started in earnest. The new cows were not letting down all their milk yet, but we had had five gallons at the previous night's milking and six gallons that morning. The exciting part was that we could put two churns up on the stand for collection by the lorry. It was such a relief to be selling milk at last, instead of the constant cream and butter making! We also took six and a half dozen eggs to Barnstaple Pannier market to be sold on a stall. A large load of feed was delivered, and we had three power cuts; a short one in the morning, another from three to six thirty, which delayed the milking, and a third at nine o'clock, so we went to bed.

All the hens were now laying well and all three ducks had started. The milk yield had increased to sixteen and a half gallons daily, and with our first paying guest due on the 21st things were looking up.

On the 21st I was up very early cleaning, doing a batch of washing and making a steak and kidney pie for the evening meal. The nurse arrived at Umberleigh station in the afternoon and John went to fetch her. I watched eagerly as the car arrived, and was astonished to see a very black lady emerge. She was a South African named Viji. I felt a little anxious at first, as I had never met a black person before, but she was nice and very easy to get on with. She was wearing several layers of very colourful clothes. We took her down to see the cows being milked and Sam, Rosalyn and the children came across to meet her later. Unfortunately the TV packed up at six o'clock.

It was not the best time of year for a holiday in the country, especially as Viji was only here for bed and breakfast and evening meal and was supposed to entertain herself for the rest of the time. We did take her to South Molton and Barnstaple each week and for a drive across Exmoor via Porlock and Lynmouth, also to a farm sale at Chittlehampton where we bought a third calver Ayrshire for £106. We named her Henrietta. She wasn't delivered until six o'clock and the power was cut immediately, so John couldn't milk her until nine thirty.

These cuts were really affecting us. Apart from the milking our taps went dry for the first time, which was very awkward with the visitor here. Also, we were eating some of our evening meals by candlelight, which might sound quite romantic, but with the other rooms all in darkness and no TV or wireless we had little sympathy with the miners.

Viji went walking most days, but the fields and woods were so muddy that she usually managed to slip down and required a good wash or a hot bath when she returned. She was refused food in an Umberleigh pub – presumably because she was black – and had to walk a good distance to the Portsmouth Arms where she was treated more kindly.

On her tenth day here she slipped down once again and ruined her best trousers, so decided to return to London the next day. She assured us that she had enjoyed all her meals – especially the roast pheasant – but she realised that it was the wrong time of year for this type of holiday.

It was a relief to be on our own again, and we were glad that we only had one more London booking from our advert. 'We'll only have friends or family in the house in the future,' I said, and John agreed. Now we were able to concentrate fully on our farm work, and with the miners back at work we were much happier and relaxed.

Our seventh cow, Genevieve, had now been delivered. She was a big, freshly calved Ayrshire heifer from Berrynarbor. We had ordered Isabel, when she calves, from the same farm, and that would fill the shippen.

John had his last payment from the employment exchange, as he was now officially self-employed, so the cows and birds would have to support us!

John had been chain-harrowing the field recently, and

Mr Wright and Sam had been helping him with muck-spreading. In return John had been helping Sam with various jobs on his farm, and in order for him to get away early after breakfast I had been instructed in washing and sterilising the milking equipment – a lengthy and tedious job.

The weather was proving very unpredictable in March: one day warm, sunny and spring-like, while the next cold with sleet and snow. One fine morning we let the cows into Lane Field and while the Ayrshires got straight down to eating the grass, Annabel and Betsy started to gambol around and leap in the air like a couple of hyperactive children. I don't know why we thought Jerseys would be quiet and easy to control! Betsy is particularly mischievous, and it is no accident when, at milking times, she flips her tail and removes John's clean white hat each time he passes near her!

The clocks went forward last night and we didn't know! We were expecting Will, my previous boss, and his wife, Gwyneth, to visit, so John was getting the churns up early – or so he thought. To his surprise the lorry was already there to collect, and the driver mentioned the time change. We had a rush then to get through our necessary chores before our friends arrived, but we made it.

We had several more visitors arriving – some unexpectedly – all curious to know what Kinnings was like and how we were getting on. The usual remark was, 'Isn't it lovely, this is something we've always wanted to do.' I could never encourage anyone unless they had a separate income, for it took courage and a little foolhardiness to take this risk.

However, all in all we were very happy, despite minor

setbacks, and it was relaxing to walk around admiring all the wild flowers on the banks; snowdrops, primroses, purple orchids and violets, also crowds of daffodils, obviously planted at some time. We saw so many colourful birds on our walks, including jays, pheasants, woodpigeons, goldcrests, goldfinches, bullfinches, buzzards, swallows and house martins. At dusk we saw a barn owl flying in and out of the barn, and during the night we heard other owls hooting in the distance. Several herons were nesting at the top of the trees below our meadow and we heard them shrieking after dark – a very weird sound. The foxes also disturbed us in the night with the vixens screaming at intervals. It was all very different from town life.

The family were with us for Easter. Iain was soon busy with the tractor again and doing repairs to our A40. He was very useful to us on these visits. Michael and Maggie enjoyed collecting the eggs, and we were now averaging twenty-four daily. I pickled some in vinegar but sold most, and Maggie took five-dozen home with her, as well as a pound of cream.

After they left John put seeds in the garden, which Sam had ploughed in readiness. He sowed peas, carrots, parsley, spring onions and parsnips, and earlier had planted onion sets, spring cabbages, broad beans and early potatoes, so we were going to be self sufficient for vegetables.

The cows had had their annual tuberculosis test and when the vet came to check them after three days they all passed. Aunty Edie came to stay for twelve days, and was then going on to another friend. She was remarkably active for an eighty-year-old, and insisted on working around the farm, chopping wood, helping to clear brambles and having a bonfire. She also helped me in the house, did some sewing and knitted a pair of socks for John within a week! She said that keeping busy took her mind off losing Bob.

Mr Wright and Sam were now ploughing the meadow for us, as the grass there was in a poor state. Once ploughed it has to be dragged, limed, rolled and finally sown with grass seed. It took several days to complete, but was well worth the effort. Seven weeks later the grass had grown nicely, but it required Sam to bring over his sheep for a day to firm down the new grass, as the heavy cows would have damaged it.

We now had some very bad luck with our transport. The A40 packed up completely; first and reverse gears had gone and we couldn't get it up the lane. Sam lent us his tractor and link box to transport our three churns of milk. We decided a van would be useful for us and we managed a part exchange with a Commer diesel, a 20 cwt van – a fatal mistake! In the ensuing weeks it refused to go up our lane, required a new heavy-duty battery, the radiator boiled over scalding John's arm, it caught fire twice – a pity we didn't let it burn out and claim the insurance money – kept refusing to start, spilt diesel on the road, started smoking, had a second-hand gear box fitted and finally our heavy entrance gate swung to in the wind, bashed the back of it and smashed the lights. That was the end. We couldn't sell it, so we then used it as a store for bags of feed etc.

One day a man noticed it near the gate and wanted to convert it into a motor camper. He said he knew all about these vans and would have no trouble with the mechanics. We were so glad to see the back of it and to get a little money back. We never heard the outcome!

In the meantime John bought a Morris 1000 to save us from borrowing Sam's car, and a churn carrier to take up the milk.

Our busiest time in the house that year was the spring Bank Holiday. Previous neighbours of ours – Carol, Rodney and their three young sons, –had booked for three days. The London couple with baby Jake were to stay for a week, but they weren't arriving until the Sunday. Our family had decided to try out the caravan for the weekend, so we had many preparations to make. We put three single beds in one room for the boys. There were double beds in the other two rooms and a cot for the baby. John and I had to fix up something for ourselves in our top living room.

The couple with Jake turned up at eight o'clock on Sunday morning while we, after milking, were trying to snatch a quick meal before cooking breakfast for Carol and family. Little Jake was about a year old and a very happy child, but his mother was rather quiet and looked tired – probably from having travelled overnight. She asked for his milk and water to be boiled and seemed nervy.

Unfortunately it was a very blustery day with frequent showers and there was a poor forecast with gales for the next day. Nevertheless, it was a terrible shock when early the next morning the father announced that they were going home! He assured us it was nothing to do with us, but said his wife was poorly following an operation, couldn't cope with the baby and the weather, and was worried that Jake had disturbed people by crying in the night – actually nobody heard a sound. He insisted on paying for the week, and although I made a half-hearted protest, it was a great relief to us as we had gone to some expense in preparing for them. It certainly strengthened our resolve to have no more strangers staying in the house.

The Tuesday – and indeed the rest of the week – was fine and sunny, but our remaining visitors had to return home for work.

When I started the big wash the pump motor packed up. We phoned SWEB, who sent a man quickly to collect the motor for repair. He returned with it next afternoon, but we had been without water all the morning, having had no means of pumping water from the well. The man suggested we buy another motor as a standby, which turned out to be very good advice.

At least John – inadvertently – caused us a few laughs. He was busy with DIY jobs in the kitchen and was sawing a piece of wood when he accidentally sawed off the corner of a kitchen chair! He then started to fix laminate on the kitchen table, but snapped the first piece and had to get another. Unfortunately he cracked the corner of that, so he rounded off the table to match!

On a glorious June day Sam cut the grass for hay in Well Field in view of a favourable forecast for the next few days. We kept our fingers crossed. Sam said it was the longest, heaviest grass he'd ever cut. The next day we actually had some rain at about eleven o'clock and it was much cooler and very depressing. John turned the grass twice and helped Sam with shearing his sheep. The third day was fine and sunny again, and it was the same forecast for the day after that, so we booked Mr Murch to come and bale. The forecast let us down again, as it was mainly dull with just a short burst of sun. However, the grass was baled – although rather green – and it was just as well, as it rained on and off for the next four days. We had 229 bales. Ten days later we cut the bottom half of Hill Field on a warm, sunny day. We then had showers and bright intervals for the next seven days, but on the eighth day it dried well and was baled in the evening: 211 bales. We did not enjoy haymaking; it was too nerve-racking with this weather!

Our last hay was made in dry, sunny weather, although there were a few spots of rain on the day we baled. We had only 134 bales from Lane Field, as it had not been set off for long. Thank goodness it was all over for another year!

We were very disappointed with our May milk cheque, received towards the end of June. The price was down from 19 to 16 pence per gallon, so although we sent off more milk than in April we had less money.

The first people came to the caravan – a very pleasant couple who thoroughly enjoyed their week. The caravan was booked for seven weeks this year. We had to turn away many enquiries for the same weeks. It was certainly successful and less traumatic than catering for people in the house!

One man arrived with his children, Duncan and Delia. They had great fun flying a kite over Kinnings. The children fell in love with Charlie cockerel and the hens, and when they called Charlie he would walk up the lane to them, obviously to receive a titbit. One of the hens allowed Duncan to pick her up each day, and there was quite a sad farewell when they had to leave.

In mid-July I had a very difficult time with visitors – especially as John was spending a considerable amount of time helping Sam. The family turned up on the Friday evening to stay until Monday. Mr and Mrs Cole and their two daughters came to the caravan on Saturday. On

Sunday Margaret and Dorothy and two friends came for the day. It was all very enjoyable, but I still had to welcome Aunty Edie and her friend Norma, who were due the next day to stay for a week!

Monday was a fine, warm day, and I was expecting Edie and Norma for lunch, as well as the friend who was driving them up from Weymouth, which meant five for the meal. I decided to make a steak and kidney pie first and then prepare the vegetables. Time was racing on. The family had gone out somewhere, so I stripped their bed, made up two beds for the ladies and cleaned upstairs. Then I had to empty wardrobes and drawers and find space for the contents in our room, which meant rushing up and down the long passage and occasional journeys down the narrow winding staircase to the kitchen to keep an eye on the cooking. I was exhausted and they were due any minute. Fortunately, John turned up first and almost immediately a car came down the drive. We watched in horror as three ladies stepped out followed by a man!

'Who on earth is that?' I asked John. 'I haven't cooked enough for six!'

'It will be all right,' he assured me, but it wasn't. Five average servings stretched into six meant opening a large tin of peas, and so far as I was concerned the whole meal was spoilt. The family turned up in the middle of it and had to cater for themselves in the kitchen – I was beyond caring. Mrs Richards and her man friend, who had come along as company for her on the way home but hadn't bothered to phone us and let us know, departed mid-afternoon, but not before she had gone upstairs to inspect the bedrooms. It was like matron looking for a speck of dust! Finally she twitched the curtains in one room and the lot fell down!

We bought two more cows, the first a Jersey X from Sam on a week's trial. If she came up to four gallons a day we would keep her. She managed it, so we did. We called her Delilah. Later on we had Molly – a freshly calved heifer from Berrynarbor – making ten cows in all. We had worked hard restoring the old shippen for use, so when it was time for the cows to be tied in at night we would have three to go in there. They would be dried off in readiness for calving in a couple of months' time.

On August 22nd Dad came to stay. Unfortunately we had a severe water shortage as the weather had been hot and sunny day after day – why couldn't this happen at haymaking time? We had to get two elsan closets and put in the pigsties. We took him to South Molton sheep fair, which is reputed to be the largest in the country. I think he was worried about the water situation, and went to stay with Uncle Ken for eleven days. Actually, uncle has similar trouble with his well, but he hasn't any cows to milk, which takes up a great quantity of water.

On September 5th we had the great news that Maggie had had a baby girl, Catherine Mary – 7 lbs 14 oz. – and both were well. She was our second grandchild, and we couldn't wait to see her. We managed to visit on the 12th, borrowing Sam's car for the journey. It was lovely to see them all, especially baby Catherine, who was getting on nicely, and Michael, who was very excited by our visit. We were back home in good time for milking, and John shot a decent-sized rabbit in the evening – his fourth that year. Shandy had left a dead, full-sized rat outside the back door.

Clarice and Bill arrived on the 16th. They were ex-neighbours and very good friends of ours. It was so nice to see them again, but we were shocked by Clarice's state of health. We hadn't realised she had been so ill. When we saw her two days before we moved to Kinnings she had hugged me and said she was so sorry we were leaving.

They went off each day visiting Westward Ho!, Ilfracombe, Woolacombe and Bideford, and we had cosy chats with them after their evening meal. They returned home on the 21st and we never saw dear Clarice again.

One day John helped Mr Wright pick his peas and runner beans for the market. In the evening we were allowed to pick any that were left for ourselves. We found several pounds, which we prepared for the freezer. Together with our own veg, blackberries, strawberries, gooseberries and blackcurrants, apples from Sam, mushrooms and hazelnuts, we were doing very well, even better with our own milk and eggs, rabbits, ducks and chicken. Whatever problems we encountered we were certainly not going to starve! There were two apple trees remaining in our orchard, bearing small green cookers, which made delicious apple jelly.

Myra came to stay for two weeks in early October. She is an old school friend. We were at boarding school together and have remained close friends ever since. During the war I stayed with her on her father's dairy farm, so this was a visit in reverse. We went for good long walks, and most days it stayed fine. We picked more blackberries, went to the river, through Sam's marshes and the woods. Some afternoons we had a cooking session – Myra was a wonderful cook and made especially lovely shortbread. She had brought her cat with her on this occasion, a pretty black cat called Suzie. Where she was living at present it was not safe for Suzie, and she wondered if we would keep her on the farm. I wasn't too keen as she was very, very nervous and Shandy wasn't very keen on her, but I decided to try it out. Myra also helped me tidy up the front garden and the rockery, and when she finally left I felt quite lonely.

One day Annabel and Delilah jumped the fence by the shippen. We couldn't understand why, especially when Delilah gave no milk at all in the afternoon. We heard afterwards that the Tiverton Hunt had passed through the adjoining field, with hunting horn and dogs barking, and this had obviously terrified them. We hoped that Annabel had not injured her calf, which was due in about seven weeks. Wretched hunting!

John had made an entrance into Well Field from the lane. It cut through the middle of the garden, so had to be fenced off. It saved having to drive up the lane into Hill Field and then down Hill Field and into Well.

On 10th November the family came again for a week, but what terrible weather for them! It was so disappointing, as we were getting more rain than we needed that month.

Catherine was growing well, and Michael was still 'helping' Granddad whatever the weather. Suzie cat was being very difficult with extra people about. Maggie and I went to a Tupperware party with Rosalyn one evening, but apart from that it was a fairly uneventful week. Never mind – they were coming for Christmas that year from the 23rd to the 27th of December. We were looking forward to that.

In early December John had an interview for a part-time job at a nearby feed mill. The hours were from one thirty to five o'clock five days a week. It would help out, as we had lots of unexpected expenses. He started on 4th December, a day of gales, hailstones, thunder and lightning. He arrived home just before five thirty. When he started to milk Molly the electricity failed about halfway through and was off for nearly three hours. The rest didn't get milked that night.

On the 6th Annabel started to calve in the afternoon, so I had to call Sam and Mr Wright. She took her time over it, and I think she was nervous in a fresh place and without John. However, a bull calf arrived at five o'clock and John arrived home from work when it was all over. It was a good strong calf.

We had a shock on the 14th when, after tea, John discovered Annabel lying on the floor of the Shippen unable to get up and very swollen. He sent for the vet, who came quickly and treated her for milk fever, which was a new thing for us. Fortunately she was soon on her feet again, but John checked on her at ten thirty and again at two, just to be sure.

John broke up for Christmas on the 22nd and was pleasantly surprised to receive a £1 Christmas box, extra to pay.

Carol singers came round – about twenty of them – and we were sorry our family were not here in time for that. They turned up on the 23rd. The children had slight colds, but otherwise were well.

We were very disappointed at not receiving all our usual cards. There was to be no further delivery until the 27th. Actually, we received five on the 28th and three more on the 29th. These three were posted on the 18th! Not like the old days when we had a Christmas Day delivery…

Christmas Day was fine after a damp start. We opened our presents after breakfast. Michael was quite excited, but behaved well. Iain's 11 lb 10 oz turkey was very enjoyable (a gift from Imperial in lieu of tobacco). John helped me with the cooking, so I felt more relaxed this visit. It was good to have him available for a change. We all went to admire Sammy calf in the afternoon. He was really lively and strong and enjoyed all the attention.

On Boxing Day we all walked across to Rosalyn's in the afternoon carrying baby Catherine. Mrs Wright came across to see her. John took Michael to see Sam's calves and his first lamb of the season.

John went back to work on the 27th and the family returned home in the afternoon. Suzie was pleased to have her tea in peace – she had been eating in the outhouse for the last couple of days! It is a shame she is such a timid little creature.

So, another year had ended, and we spent time going through the pros and cons. The cows had done well on the whole, except for the loss of Clara. There had been the occasional case of mastitis or of ovaries not working, but the vets had quickly rectified these. The trouble was that after injections we had to hold back the milk for four days. We had passed our tuberculosis and brucellosis tests. The hens and ducks had done well for us. We had missed one occasionally, possibly to a fox. The caravan had been a success. We had been fortunate to have good neighbours. Our main problem had been lack of water, which occurred each time we had a long spell of fine weather. Another thing was the van fiasco, but we had seen the back of that. The power cuts were worrying in February, but that was a one off. We decided it had been quite a good year, and were optimistic that things could only get better.

We had become accustomed to living in North Devon now. We understood the language at last. They say 'Us is going to market.' A young girl is 'little maid'. The Alder tree is 'Aller'. Hay bailed while still damp is 'master green'. Thistles are 'dashels' and gorse is called by the old English name 'furze'. Hoggs – year old lambs – are 'ugs'. Running may be 'rinning'. This or that is 'thic and thicy', pronounced as in the. Shaking hands is a usual habit, one long since discontinued in the Bristol area. In shops selling farming equipment and animal feed we would be asked if we wanted to pay or book it, even though we were complete strangers to them! Everywhere we found helpfulness, kindness and friendliness, and we loved it.

Chapter III
1973

We started 1973 with high hopes of overcoming our water shortage. We had written to the North Devon Water Board to enquire about mains water. Our hopes were dashed when they replied at the end of January saying that they could only connect us if we were near the council houses, and as we were over a mile from them there was no chance.

The cows had started calving at regular intervals, and their calves were fetching good prices at market – £65 was the best for a Charolais X Ayrshire. Most gave good milk yields with the exception of Delilah, who was very poor this time, and Molly who had summer mastitis and lost one quarter. These two eventually went as barreners. Genevieve gave over seven gallons a day, and Felicity over six gallons. We bought five more cows during the year; Judy and Lucy, Guernsey heifers, Lotus and Kate from Berrynarbor, and finally Camella, a pedigree Friesian from market. She was delivered early and when we arrived home from shopping we were surprised to see her tied up in the shippen eating hay. She glanced round at us, quite unconcerned, and continued eating. She was a good cow and gave plenty of milk.

On 25th February we travelled up for Catherine's christening, which went off very well. She didn't cry throughout the service. There was a good gathering of family and friends at the house afterwards. We left at four o'clock and everything was white with snow from Taunton onwards. Fortunately this was washed away by rain the following day.

We had a surprise when we paid Sam for barley and he gave us a tame lamb, which he'd bought at market for a pound. This was very exciting. We had to feed her four times a day with a bottle of milk, which meant buying a baby's bottle and teat. We called her Tich and she was a lively little creature. When we next went to market we saw more little orphans in a pen, baaing loudly, and we couldn't resist buying another to keep Tich company. We ended up with twelve during the next few weeks, but three of them died. The tiniest ones are very vulnerable and would be better put straight onto a ewe, so we decided to look for stronger ones in future.

We had sheep coming into our meadow constantly from our other neighbour, and although we complained he did nothing about improving the hedge. We needed all the grass we could get for our cows and used fertiliser to encourage it, so we didn't want it wasted on another farmer's sheep. We tried to improve the hedge from our side, but they found a way in via the wood. One day John saw the young fellow in charge of them and went across to complain yet again, but he just jumped on his tractor and drove off!

At the same time we had Peter lamb – a tame one – coming in from Sam's side. We couldn't get rid of him, so Sam put him down in their marshes. Not content there he preferred another farmer's field and was accidentally taken to Combe Martin in a lorry, stayed there for three weeks, and then came back to pester us again!

We had been wanting to get a better tractor, and were

pleased to hear of a Fordson Dexta at Umberleigh, with a small link box, for £165. This was an improvement on our old one, which was eventually sold for scrap.

The eggs had dropped off during the winter, but by February the hens and ducks were laying again and we soon had plenty. In April we were selling twelve dozen hen eggs and two dozen duck eggs weekly, pickling some more and sitting broody hens on others. Rosalyn often had broodies, and we were both getting ducklings and chickens hatching regularly. John would kill off an older hen when it stopped laying and we would enjoy a good meal from it. I found that cooking it in the pressure cooker and then browning it in the oven made it tender and delicious.

On 1st April Margaret and Dorothy came again for the day – a cold, blustery day, which seemed to be the usual weather for our visitors, and certainly for our family. They often had a rainy week, which changed to warm and sunny as soon as they returned home. Margaret bought eight-dozen eggs and eleven ¼ lbs of cream, as she had orders from friends.

On 10th April we heard of a terrible plane crash. Several North Somerset people had set off for a day in Switzerland when the plane crashed in Basle, killing many from the Axbridge, Cheddar and Congresbury areas – including five family members of an old school friend of Maggie's. A very sad ending to their trip.

Emma gave us a shock when she calved in May, eleven days late with a very big calf. We had to get help from the vet, who injected her against milk fever, but she was unable to stand. She had to be milked from two teats lying down. The second day she was still down. The vet came again and decided her nerves had been bruised during calving. He, Sam and Mr Wright managed to drag her outside the old shippen into the fresh air. John couldn't help as he had a painful back and his doctor was arranging for him to have an x-ray. When he was trying to encourage Emma in the evening she managed to struggle up and stand for a few minutes before collapsing again. On the third day she was still down and became bloated and stiff, so back came the vet to give her more injections for milk fever. He lectured us on choosing a Charolais bull which produced large calves, although the artificial inseminator (the bull in the bowler hat, as he was jokingly called) assured us that there should be no problem as they only used semen from bulls who had been tested for easy calving. For the next five days Emma gradually improved a little more each day until on the ninth day she was able to walk down to the shippen for afternoon milking and then out into the field. Then Annabel became ill with a chill and congestion of one lung, so two more visits and injections from the vet were necessary to get her right.

The doctor signed John off work. The first x-ray didn't show anything wrong, but after tests and a second x-ray a few weeks later he was told it was degeneration of the lumber nerve, so he gave up his outside job.

We started getting busy with visitors for the spring Bank Holiday. Carol, Rodney and boys came from Friday evening until Tuesday morning. The boys gave Snow White, our smallest lamb, her bottle, and another day they had rides on Sam's pony, Beauty.

After they left on Tuesday our family arrived. Michael loved the lambs, but Catherine was still too young to appreciate them. They had the usual changeable weather and returned home on the Sunday. Shortly afterwards

Mr and Mrs Bailey and Andrew arrived for two weeks in the caravan. They had wonderful weather throughout and said when they left that it was the best holiday they had ever had. Maggie was very poorly at this time, so Michael came to stay with us for a couple of weeks, and he and Andrew had great fun together. At the same time Well Field was cut for hay and baled on the fourth day – 143 bales – and because of the lovely weather, Hill Field was cut and baled after only three days. On the final day John and I were forking the loose hay onto the rows and three-year-old Michael was helping with a tiny hayfork. We suddenly noticed him lying fast asleep between the rows, but had to disturb him quickly as Ron Murch was just arriving with the baler. There were 295 bales of excellent hay, and Mr Wright helped John carry in most of them the same evening. We had to buy in a considerable amount of hay also, but we did prefer our own. In order to make our grass go further for the cows, John now strip-grazed it, fencing off a fresh section after each milking. The cows loved this, and their milk yield certainly improved. By the time they finished a couple of fields the first section, which had been fertilised, was ready for them again.

One morning when I turned on the cold-water tap in the bathroom I noticed a foul smell and feathers started coming through the tap! The mystery was soon cleared up when John discovered a dead bird in the tank. He drained off the water and cleaned and sterilised the tank – a lengthy job. He then fixed wire netting over it to ensure it never happened again.

John was frequently having to fetch water from the river in old churns – mostly drinking water for the cows, but some to keep our cistern filled so that the flush could be pulled. When we had visitors in the house John and I used the Elsan during the day.

The caravan was booked for nine weeks during the summer and everyone seemed to enjoy themselves, although it was very basic. I think the situation appealed to them – it was within easy reach of Exmoor and the coast, with Dartmoor in the other direction.

We had more visitors staying in the house. In July Aunty Edie came with Bert and Doris, plus their dog, Chum. They expected full board, as they wanted to stay around the farm. It was dry and warm all the week, so we were anxious about water again. Also John was helping Sam with his haymaking, fetching water from the river (a time consuming job), milking cows and fencing the grazing strips. I was helping to clear up in the dairy, feeding the lambs and providing four meals instead of two. They kept saying, 'Come and sit down and talk to us,' when they were enjoying the sun in the garden!

However, Bert did do a couple of jobs for us, and one day he and Doris gave the caravan a good spring clean – including the windows – as it was unoccupied that week.

Carol and Rodney came again in July, this time for two weeks. As well as the three boys they brought Carol's mother with them. Fortunately, after breakfast they went off for the day, mainly to Woolacombe, which was their favourite, and one day they took their boat to Dawlish and Lympstone. The weather remained quite good for them, but we were pleased to get three days of heavy rain as soon as they left. Four days later Jean and Bill arrived, also ex-neighbours. It was good to hear all their news. Jean and I walked to the river in the evening and then her father joined us in the meadow where the lambs were having high jinks. Tich put a bucket round her neck – one of her favourite tricks.

During July we bought a Merry Tiller for the garden and orchard, also a second-hand ice bank cooler for cooling the milk. It had been taking so much of our precious water to cool it before and this made a great difference – especially in the hot weather.

Our family came again in August for two weeks. They were luckier than usual with the weather, heavy rain, thunder and lightning coming overnight and clearing up next day. Catherine was showing more interest in everything by then, and we looked forward to when she could run around with Michael. He was still following Granddad everywhere. One day we thought we had given him the slip, as we were about to pluck three freshly killed ducks in the utility room. He was very fond of the ducks and we thought it might upset him. Just as we had plucked the first one he turned up, looked intently at the poor bird, and amazed us by saying quite cheerfully, 'Put him down, Granddad, and see if he'll go!'

We heard that Ron Murch had some young pigs for sale, and as our piggeries were not in use now we decided we could have a couple to fatten. We took Michael with us to collect them and they were put in a sack and into the boot of the car. Halfway home, Michael, who was sitting in the back, complained that something was hurting his back. We realised that the pigs had escaped from the sack and were loose. We dared not open the boot until we arrived home, so tried to pacify Michael, assuring him that they couldn't get into the car. I wish I could have believed that myself! It was pretty hair-raising.

Those pigs turned out to be escapologists, as two days later I spotted them in the front garden. They kept getting out of their house and looked so cute walking up the lane together, but it was very difficult to get them back in, so it was a relief when John found time to make a stronger door for their sty and their daily walk was discontinued. Mr Wright and Sam helped John to ring their noses, and I went around picking up acorns for them, one of their treats.

Our lambs had grown well, in fact the largest one had already gone into the freezer. Sam had bought five others from us, leaving us with just three. One morning Larry looked very miserable and we discovered he had maggots. Flies had laid eggs on him in the humid weather and the resulting maggots were eating into his flesh. We realised now why sheep have to be dipped to keep the flies away. Sam brought over some oil and we had to pick out the wriggling maggots. It was a horrible job, and he was so badly affected – with hundreds of them – that we had to keep on having another go. We then noticed a small dark patch on each of the other two lambs, but we were able to treat them quickly. We kept Larry in a shed, but although we had now removed all the maggots we were left with a very sick lamb. Then came the miracle! He walked out from his shed, into our garden, made straight for the raspberry canes and stripped off and ate all the leaves! How he knew this was a cure was a mystery, but within hours he had improved and next day he was back with the others, his usual lively self.

We had become friendly with Joy Herniman, who we met quite frequently in the market. John had already met her and her husband, Fred, on the fox shoots, and one day she came and introduced herself to me. In September she sold a Friesian X Jersey heifer in Barnstaple for £260, and then hand-milked her into a bucket! Two weeks later her Blue Roan made £245. We were very impressed.

I was still writing a great number of letters, so was disappointed when postage went up to 3 and 3½ p having previously been 2 and 2½ p. All prices had kept rising since decimalisation.

Myra came to stay on 11th October and brought a big box of fruit and mushrooms with her. On the Sunday we took her for a drive to Appledore and Instow, and most days we went for a walk. The week passed very quickly, and I am sure Suzie missed her when she left, as Myra made a great fuss of her.

A week later Dad came to stay. He seemed poorly and was eating very little at first, but soon improved and was eager to do little jobs around the farm. After ten days he announced that he would be staying for three weeks this time! We took him to Torrington, Westward Ho!, Ilfracombe, Woolacombe and Saunton Sands and he enjoyed everything. I'm glad we didn't know then that it was to be his last visit to us.

There was an oil crisis at this time, and we were getting anxious about proposed power cuts. People were being asked not to travel in cars, and on 29th November we collected petrol coupons from the post office. On 28th December many shops in Barnstaple were without electricity, including SWEB(!), but lit by candles and oil lamps because of the present emergency. Luckily it was settled before we needed to use the coupons.

On 27th November Sam took our pigs to Yeo's Abattoir in his trailer. What a job we had to load them! It took ages, with them squealing all the time. We had had them for three months and they had reached a good weight – 103 lbs and 94 lbs dead weight. We had the smaller one back for the freezer and salted a piece of belly to use as bacon.

John went to the Goose and Gander Pub in South Molton for five weekly lectures on farm accounts. He was already doing his own income tax and VAT returns, and had also helped Rosalyn to do theirs.

On 20th December we visited Maggie in Backwell to exchange Christmas presents. They had bought a new house which they would be moving into shortly, and we were taken to see it. We had fish and chips for dinner and Michael said, 'We are in South Molton now,' remembering it was something we usually had in South Molton on market days. We were invited to Uncle Ken's on Christmas Day, but were unable to manage it until teatime. We phoned Maggie after dinner and spoke to my brother, Iain's parents and Michael. It was a beautiful sunny day, but misty in the evening for driving home across the moor.

So ended another busy and eventful year.

Chapter IV
1974

January 1974 started with terrible weather, all heavy rain and gales. The roof was lifted off a calf house one night and had to be firmly secured. Fortunately there was no calf in there. The river was rising fast and the fields were saturated. Sam had some sheep in a field on the other side of the river, and they had to be brought back via the road with John, Sam and his father walking with them and Rosalyn driving the car. Several trees fell in the wood as a result of the gales, one falling partially into Meadow. This came in useful for the fires. Betsy calved in January – a good bull calf. Unfortunately prices were down in the market and he only fetched £29 on 1st February. This was the start of a bad month for us.

John took our lambs, Larry and Snow White, to Yeo's Abattoir in the back of the car after first removing the back seat. It was heartbreaking to watch them go off like a couple of happy kids with Larry looking out through the window at me. I thought I had become hardened since losing Clara, but the tears fell again. Soon after this we heard that Yeo's had gone bankrupt, or 'squit', as they say in north Devon, so we were unlikely to get any money for our lambs. We applied to the official receiver just in case, but were unlucky.

We had four cows due to calve during February. Henrietta was first with a heifer calf, then Caroline with a bull, both without problems. Next came Genevieve with a beautiful black and white bull calf, although we had hoped for a heifer to keep. We had a terrible shock next day finding him lying out and bloated, and by evening looking almost dead. We rang the vet, but he didn't come, just advised us to give him Epsom salts. He was worse the next morning so we rang the vet again. Mr Wilson, our reliable favourite, came and said he had a twisted gut and nothing could be done. He died soon after and was collected for the hunt kennels.

On wet days we were busy painting in the house and caravan and John made two strong doors for the piggeries, which we intended to use as calf houses. We had had enough of pigs for the time being!

Felicity calved at the end of February. At last a beautiful black and white heifer, Sally, who we would keep.

March and April were gardening months, and for rolling grass and spreading fertiliser in the fields. We had bought fourteen lambs and they were keeping us busy with four feeds a day, although four of these died. Isobel had a Hereford heifer calf on 19th March.

On 30th April John collected Aunty Edie from Weymouth to stay with us for two weeks. Bantie was out from her secret nest with eight strong chicks. She was a nervy, wild bird and easily took fright, which caused the chicks to scatter. One disappeared and was never seen again. Another time she surprised us by flying through the air, missing Aunty's head by a couple of inches and giving her a nasty shock. A couple of days later Bantie went berserk and deserted her chicks, so John put them with a grey broody in the run he had set up in the front garden. Shandy still managed to jump in and catch and eat one little chick, which was very upsetting. We didn't mind him catching the rats or even the moles – his latest feat. These can make a terrible mess of a field with all the molehills, and we had already borrowed a trap from Uncle Ken and managed to catch one. Shandy, however, had proudly displayed two dead ones, one in the kitchen and one outside the back door, and we had no further trouble from them.

The milk was being collected at seven forty-five these days, so John had to be up just after five o'clock to get the five churns on the stand in time.

We had a fresh problem with the lambs. They are getting orf – horrible crusty scabs around their mouths. John and I both had it on our thumbs, and it throbbed and was extremely painful. We were told that it may have been in the woodwork around the farm, left from the previous farmer's sheep. It was certainly very contagious and not easy to treat. Eventually a neighbouring farmer gave us a bottle of liquid to inject into them, and this was more successful than anything we had tried before.

We ordered a greenhouse from Mole Valley Farmers, which had to be assembled and foundations prepared. It took a long time, but was well worth it as we grew loads of sweet flavoured tomatoes and enormous cucumbers.

On Friday 24th May the family arrived. Michael and Catherine were excited and played outside and it was nice to see them running around together.

We were very worried about Emma, who should have calved a few days before. Her udder was huge and John had to milk her to make her more comfortable. We had opted for a Devon calf this time, which should prove easy after the trouble she had with the Charolais the year before.

The Sunday was a disastrous day in spite of being

sunny and warm. First of all the tractor wouldn't start so the churns had to be taken up in the car. After breakfast we had a phone call to say that John's father had passed away during the night, peacefully in his sleep. Later on the police rang, also the funeral director. It was a terrible morning, but more was yet to come. We struggled through Sunday dinner, trying to be bright for the sake of the children. Then we all walked down to the meadow for another inspection of Emma. We could see her lying down there with a calf nearby. Another shock! The calf was still in the bag and dead. Emma had obviously not felt well enough to release it. She was having difficulty getting up and needed a calcium injection from the vet, but was eventually back to normal.

The next couple of weeks were hectic. John made visits to Keynsham to see Dad's solicitor and the registrar, and John and Iain went to the funeral at Bath Crematorium, while Maggie and I stayed home with the children. John was fetching water from the river every other day. We visited Uncle Ken regarding his brother's death. Kirkhams came to fit new front tyres to the tractor. We exchanged our Morris 1000 for a Ford Anglia. We started haymaking in Well Field.

As it was going to be difficult for John to get away now, we arranged for me to stay with Maggie for a few days so that we could sort things out in Dad's house. The day I went there was a torrential thunderstorm, and John rang in the evening to say the hay grass had got very wet and the shippen and dairy were flooded with muddy water. The next two days were fine and the bales were brought in, but rather green as usual. The same happened with the Hill Field hay. Thank goodness our haymaking was over for this year!

We were disgusted to hear that postage had gone up to 3½ and 4½ p when I was writing more letters than ever.

Maggie and I had a busy time at Keynsham, sorting Dad's clothes and furniture and cleaning out generally, but there was plenty left to do. John managed three more visits in spite of going to Sam's for four days helping with haymaking and packing wool. At last everything was clear for the surplus furniture to be collected and the house put up for sale.

We had more day visits from Margaret and Dorothy and Jean and Bill, and now in July the caravan folk were arriving, which made extra work. The first couple arrived with a four-year-old boy and a dog. Very pleasant people. They left on Friday evening, apologising for their son spilling tea over a cover. This meant washing the cover, drying and ironing it and replacing it in time for the next arrivals in the morning. We also discovered a broken spring in the mattress. We turned it over and kept our fingers crossed, and luckily no one complained!

The third family who came were a real problem. They booked as a couple with three children and assured us that one was a baby and they would provide her bed, as the caravan only slept four. Baby turned out to be five years old! They had travelled from the East Coast in an ancient three-wheeler, which didn't like our narrow road with grass sticking up in the middle, or indeed, our steep, stony lane.

Our own family were staying with us this week, which was fortunate, as the three-wheeler wouldn't start on Monday. Iain took the father to the nearest garage for petrol and then had to ring the AA for assistance. John put their battery on charge on Tuesday night. More trouble with the three-wheeler on Wednesday and John had to take him to the garage for a part. On Thursday they actually went to Woolacombe, but there were heavy showers and thunder. On the Friday their car had to be towed up the lane and they left for home after nine o'clock with the wife asking if we would have them again next year. I managed to smile, but did not reply!

All the week they had been using us as a shop, saying, 'Put it on the bill', so their cheque was well in excess of the rental. The shock came ten days later when the cheque was re-presented by our bank. When this happened a second time we were really worried. John remembered that the wife was a nurse and worked out when her pay would be going into her bank, so we put their cheque in for the third time to coincide with this, and this time we were lucky. I'm afraid they had no intention of paying us.

Because they left so late on the Friday night I had to leave the cleaning for the next morning. I was up very early, and having washed my hair I started on the van, which certainly needed plenty of cleaning. There I was in overall and rollers, looking a real Mrs Mop, when I was horrified to see the next people arriving very early. At least this was a pleasant family, and I was very sorry that they had rain every day. They were so fed up that they decided to go home early on Friday morning, and of course this turned out to be a warm, sunny day.

The next couple and their son came without a car. I did my best to put them off as we were so isolated, but they insisted on booking and appeared to enjoy their week.

All this time we were busy as usual on the farm with cows and lambs and hens, also gardening and picking blackcurrants and strawberries. I was busy in the house making jams and chutney, as well as the everyday cooking and baking.

We took four lambs to John Hill's abattoir at the end of June and three more a few days later. One of these, Jack, we wanted back and he must have heard John saying this, because as soon as he was tagged he jumped back into our car. The chap was most amused. 'This one doesn't want to stay with us,' he said.

A few days later when John went to collect him for the freezer he discovered Jack had been sent off in a lorry, supposedly by mistake. However, we heard later he had been included in a batch of small lambs especially ordered by a London hotel. We were given a lamb in place of Jack, but it wasn't like our own. That was the last lamb we would send to them!

Calf prices had plunged in the market. Lucy had a Devon heifer calf on 24th July, and Judy a Friesian bull calf on 15th August. These were good strong calves, but only fetched £8 each. In September Camella had a very good Friesian bull, which managed to fetch £26 – about half of last year's price. In October a strong bull calf from Lotus made only £2.50. The same day several bulling and in-calf Jersey heifers fetched from only £7 each. This is the down side of farming: however much an animal – or milk – costs to produce, the farmer has no say on the price he gets but has to rely entirely on market prices. We realised it would be pure luck if we made any money that year, especially as the self-employed insurance stamp had just gone up as well as the postage rates.

I was getting very irritable at times, mainly because John was spending so much time helping Sam. In July he helped for fourteen out of sixteen days, his two 'free' days being Sundays when Mr Wright did not approve of working. We couldn't go to the local flower show as John was turning grass in the marshes, and I was constantly urging him to Snowcem the side and back of the house. We had been there for almost three years and had never managed more than the front! Actually, John had more than enough of his own jobs without Sam and me playing tug of war with him! I did appreciate that Sam and Mr Wright had helped us very much in our early days here, but I felt John had easily repaid them by now, and I was worried about his troublesome back if he overdid things.

In August Rosalyn had a baby boy, Stephen, a brother for Samantha and Christopher.

John did manage to finish the painting and Snowcem, and at one stage Maggie was on the roof holding the ladder firm! Iain repaired the tractor, mower and Merry Tiller. There was usually something waiting when they came to stay.

We sent two of our best milkers as barreners in October. Emma, who had had seven calves and had serious trouble calving the last two it was pointless to get in calf again. Felicity, who had just returned the fourth time from the AI and who had calved six and a half months ago went with her. We immediately bought three heifers at market – two Friesians and a Guernsey. One was from Joy Herniman and another from Denzil Waldron, both friends of ours.

In November Joy and Fred came one afternoon to look around and to see their heifer, who they had reared as a calf, but she decided to ignore them.

By the end of November Dad's house had finally sold and we received the final account and cheque from his solicitor. His will had included several bequests – one quite large – and after all the expenses were settled the residue came to John. We felt very sad that we would not see him here again as we enjoyed his visits so much, just as he did. Maggie was not included in the will, but we put that right.

We were invited to Uncle Ken's for Christmas Day, but had to refuse as Annabel and Betsy were due to calve. Instead we met them in South Molton on Christmas Eve to exchange gifts.

Christmas Day was wet and windy all day – really miserable – and three of the cows were glum and off their food. Apart from a long chat on the phone with Maggie and the children, it was not a good day.

On 31st December we decided to purchase a 1968 David Brown tractor, as they allowed us a reasonable amount for exchanging with the Dexta. This cheered us up a little at the end of a rather disappointing year.

Chapter V
1975

1975 was an exciting year with so many new happenings. The usual things were much the same, with gales and heavy storms during January. Calf prices remained very low – one sold for 5p and two others for 50p and 75p in the market – not ours, I hasten to add. Prices did not start to improve until September. This was bad news for dairy farmers, as they rely upon this income in addition to selling milk. Cows need to calve every year to be viable, and they go dry about three months before calving. They still have to be fed during this period, and the calf price helps to offset this.

We had thirteen cows calve without mishaps this year, which was good. Unfortunately we had to send five cows out as barreners – three through low milk yields or difficulty in getting in calf, Lucy in March, who aborted at five months, and Amber in November for a different reason. She was scouring about a week after calving and not very lively. Five weeks later she was scouring badly again, losing weight and giving no milk. The vet gave her a good examination but could find nothing obviously wrong. He gave her various drenches and sent blood samples for tests without any result. We had recently bought a medical book for farm animals, dealing with diseases etc., and we thought her symptoms indicated Johnes disease. When we mentioned this, the vet immediately sent off blood and dung samples to test for it. We isolated Amber and John disinfected the milking shippen. Three days later we heard the tests were positive for Johnes disease, and Amber had to go.

The caravan was only booked for two weeks this year as we had decided not to advertise it. The curtains and covers were starting to wear out and we were finding it difficult to cope with the extra work. Luckily both families were normal this time and caused us no trouble!

We heard in January that the lady in the manor house had sixteen acres for rent at Collins – these being fields the other side of Mr Wright's farm and not far along the road from us. I rang her to enquire about this and our name was passed on to her agent. We knew several others were after it and didn't think we had much chance, so imagine our delight when on 20th February we were told we could take the tenancy from Lady Day, 25th March! Now we could really expand. The fields were mainly steep and full of weeds and brambles, so we had plenty of work there. However, there was a stream running along the bottom, which saved John having to carry water.

We were buying more machinery at this time: a roller, dung-spreader, acrobat, fertiliser spreader, rotary mower, second tractor and small bale trailer – all second hand, of course, and set against tax. We also exchanged our car for a Hillman Minx Estate, as we needed something more reliable. Now we realised that if we were to increase our cow numbers we needed another decent building, and we were fortunate to see just what we wanted, advertised at a special price. It was a Henry Plumb cubicle house with sleep/feed cubicles for twenty cows. Having decided to buy this we now had to get a firm to level out the ground and prepare the foundations.

In the meantime Maggie had a birthday and did not

receive our card – posted first class. We were furious, as a few days before the postage rates had increased to 5½ and 7 p. The service was most unreliable.

The last few days of March were very cold, with snow pitching and heavy frost at night. On Easter Sunday it rained which cleared the snow but brought fresh trouble when our pump packed up at bath time. We rang Mr Boucher, our plumber, and true to his promise he came willingly to fit a reconditioned pump. The cold weather continued for several days with alternating wintry showers and sunny periods.

John managed to spread dung and fertiliser and started rolling the fields. He had Kinnings and Collins fields to deal with now, and what with rotavating the garden and orchard ready for planting, clearing slurry, milking cows, helping me with the lambs, fetching water, doing Sam's VAT as well as ours and income tax and endless other jobs it seemed all work and no play.

The most irritating thing was the constant appearance of someone else's sheep and bullocks upsetting our animals and churning up our fields. However much we complained nothing was done to contain them on their own land.

April was a happier month. We were now exchanging visits with Joy and Fred, which we found very enjoyable. I was invited to Joan Baker's Tupperware party; a pleasant evening, and she provided a delicious selection of fancy cakes, all homemade. I received a Calor gas cooker for my birthday present, as the element on the big ring of the Baby Belling had packed up. We didn't want to light the Rayburn on warmer days, as the kitchen became so hot with our low ceilings. I was delighted to be cooking with gas, and it would be useful in the event of power cuts. All our cows were tested this month and found to be free of TB.

We applied to the Ministry of Agriculture for a grant towards the cost of the cubicle house. There was some doubt about this at first, as we were a small concern and had to show we would be viable. We had to agree to have twenty cows and to buy in store sheep in the winter months and the grant was finally approved.

In May we were working hard at Collins, getting rid of brambles and burning the bracken. We were pulling out the bracken by hand – a backbreaking job, but it is poisonous to animals, and we needed to get rid of it. The grass was beginning to grow well.

On 24th May Iain's mother died after a long illness. Next day we collected the children to stay with us. They were both packed and ready, and even Catherine was very excited. 'I'm going farming,' she announced, importantly. 'I'm going to milk the "tows" and the lambs.'

One day we took them to Withypool with a picnic tea. They loved the stepping-stones on the River Barle, and Michael managed to fall in!

Late on Friday evening Maggie and Iain arrived and the following morning we all had fun and games getting the cows to Collins for the first time. They ran along the road like mad things, and would have finished up in the village had someone not been far enough ahead to direct them into the field via Gypsy Lane. Luckily they were more sedate on the way home. It was always a traumatic event taking them along the road. When they were in a leisurely mood and ambled along, stopping for grass from the banks, we were sure to have an impatient motorist stuck behind them. Even worse were cars coming towards them and turning them around, which I found quite alarming, as I was the one walking behind. On a very hot day the cowpats caused the tarmac to rise in the road, and I was always afraid someone would complain, but by the next day it had flattened out again, so all was well.

The best time was walking without the cows, when we had left them at Collins or were on the way to collect them. Then we were relaxed and able to appreciate the sweet scent of wild honeysuckle in the hedgerows, admire the primroses, violets and many other flowers peeping through the grass on the banks, and in September we would be able to sample the blackberries. This was one of the pleasures I shall always remember.

Shandy was being very busy. He had caught at least six rats around this time. We had our May milk cheque for £550 – the largest yet. The weather was perfect for our haymaking for a change. We had received the planning permission for our building, and things were going well.

5th June was referendum day, to vote if we should stay in the Common Market. John and I voted yes, because we were assured it would help farmers. Indeed the 'Yes' vote was 2-1 to stay in. Looking back now, many years later, we feel that the British gained little from it!

The whole of June was dry and warm – some days being extremely hot. This was excellent for haymaking, and we had help from Joy and Fred, Christopher, Stephen and Janet. They would help us bring in the bales in the evenings, and we would finish up with jolly suppers in the kitchen. We made hay in Lane and Hill Fields and two of Collins fields. One afternoon in Lane Field a whirlwind lifted some of our hay, took it high in the air and scattered it in all directions. Two days later the same thing happened in Hill Field, but this time far more hay went even higher, like a great parachute, and disappeared into the distance. Someone must have been surprised where it landed!

I had a nasty shock one morning when I saw John overturn the tractor in our lane. By the time I reached it he was crawling out – luckily unhurt but for a few bruises. Murch's sent up a winch to right it and we rang re. insurance.

In mid-June a man started digging out the site for the cubicle house. Then the concrete was laid ready for erection. The building was delivered in sections, and erection commenced on 30th June and was finished on 3rd of July. It looked very good. Next the path from the house to the shippen and to the cubicle house beyond was concreted and gates were fixed.

The hot dry weather continued until 8th July, ending with the usual thunderstorm. How we needed that rain! Apart from John's frequent daily journeys to the river for water, we had no grass and were having to feed our newly made hay to the cows. It was kind of David's father to allow John to drive through his fields to the river.

The first time I visited Mrs Harris was when we went to look at David's cubicle house. She invited me into the kitchen and we sat in front of the fire with an elderly dog, now retired from farm duties. Rather foolishly I spoke to the dog, 'And how old are you?' I asked.

To my embarrassment, a voice replied 'I'm seventy!' Fortunately she was a very sweet person, and I decided not to tell her I was speaking to the dog. I quickly announced my age to make it appear that the exchange of ages was commonplace on first acquaintance. I never did

73

discover the age of the dog! We became very good friends and were soon on Christian-name terms – Beth and Mary.

In September Camella was giving eight gallons a day. She was definitely our best milker. On 10th John collected Aunty Edie from Weymouth and she stayed for two weeks. We spent a considerable time picking blackberries and cutting mushrooms from Collins. One field had dozens of 'fairy rings', each covered in mushrooms, and we were gathering them by the bucket full. Being so fresh they were delicious to eat, and we froze plenty for later on. We prepared them for cooking and then open-froze them on trays and finally bagged them up. Eventually we were giving lots to friends and neighbours. Although we always found mushrooms each year, there was never such a harvest as in 1975.

John received a summons for Jury Service. He wrote excusing himself because he was single-handed on the farm, and this was accepted.

In October we were pleasantly surprised to receive the following letter:

Dear Sir,

A review of our laboratory records shows that throughout the past year your results have met all required standards concerning milk quality.

May I congratulate you and thank you very much for your cooperation.

Yours faithfully

UNIGATE FOODS LIMITED

On 26th October the cows moved into the cubicle building for the first time. Some were nervous of putting their heads through the 'tombstone barriers' for hay, and so ate straw from their beds instead!

Between October and November John went on a five-week sheep course, one day a week at various farms, including Denzil's. Earlier in the year he had attended a dairy course.

Betsy and Annabel were both due to calve at the end of November. We had them next to each other in the old shippen, separated by a partition. On the 30th we found Annabel with her calf, but she appeared to be ignoring it. Betsy was mooing loudly and seemed very distressed, and it soon became evident that it was Betsy's calf! During calving she must have put her backside against the partition and dropped the calf in with Annabel. It was a lively little heifer, and none the worse for the experience. We called her Lulu and decided to rear her. It was four days later when Annabel started to calve at ten o'clock. John had to send for the vet, Mr McPhee, as the calf was coming backwards and upside down. It was a good-sized bull calf. Annabel needed treatment for milk fever next morning.

We bought two heifers at Barnstaple market on 28th November, making nine cows altogether purchased during 1975.

In December we had rain coming through the roof and needed repairs to the chimneystacks. More expense.

The family turned up on 20th December for a shorter visit this time. As we had no calvings imminent we were able to spend the whole of Christmas Day with Uncle Ken and Aunty Dolly, which we thoroughly enjoyed.

Mrs Parsons rang to wish us a Happy Christmas. She and the Brigadier were very friendly towards us, and we always enjoyed our chats.

So ended another eventful year.

Chapter VI
1976

January 1976 started with gales, followed by changeable weather throughout the month. Several days were mild enough to manage without heat through the day – just a small oil heater at breakfast time and a wood fire in the top room during the evenings. The thick cob walls helped to keep the rooms warm. On hot summer days they kept them cool. Cob is a strange construction of clay, stones, dried dung, straw – anything readily available for building. Kinnings is at least four hundred years old and still looks very solid. The thatch has been replaced by a slate roof.

We only bought two cows this year – second calvers from a farm sale. We were rearing our own Friesian heifer calves, and finished up with six. Lulu, Betsy's calf, was the oldest, and it was time to disbud her – that is, get rid of the little horn buds. We didn't have a holding crate at this time, so it was my job to hold her and keep her still for the anaesthetic, which proved difficult. This was followed by a sickening stench of burning horn – not a pleasant procedure, but we were determined to be independent.

We bought nineteen tame lambs in 1976, and only two died. I always bid for these at the markets. We would decide on a maximum price, and once it went over this I dropped out of the bidding. I loved carrying them out to the car, one tucked under each arm, and then choosing

Michael and Catherine feeding a calf, 1974

Michael and Catherine feeding sheep

Michael and Catherine feeding Pigs, 1978

Michael and Catherine with Percy and Polly

Lulu with Little and Large, August 1979

Maggie at the wheel, 1980

Mary, John and Bess by the River Taw, 1983

A rest from haymaking, 1983

Iain bringing in the bales, 1983

John and Roy dipping sheep, 1983

names for them. We were surprised by their intelligence, how they came to recognise their names and to respond to them. We could only bottle feed four at a time, and when the first four were finished we would stand them against the wall with their backs to us while we fed the next four. There were usually one or two inquisitive ones who peeped over their shoulders to watch, but they didn't move away. We had four back for our freezer this year and one for Maggie.

On 16th February we had our annual TB test for cows and calves. Three days later we were shocked to hear that Camella and Isobel were reactors. We were told we would get a green form preventing us from buying in or moving any cattle from the farm and this arrived four days later. Two days after this we received a pink form saying we could now move any cattle except Isobel and Camella. On 5th April these two had a further test and this time the ministry vet came to report. Isobel was now clear, but Camella was still a reactor. Again we had a green form cancelling all movements.

The ministry vet then arranged for slaughter and post-mortem, and Camella was collected on 12th April. When we had heard nothing by the 29th I rang to ask the result. I was told she was clear in the post-mortem, but now her glands would be sent for testing. In the meantime Henrietta had calved and we wanted to send her calf to market, but instead we received a licence to have him slaughtered!

It was all so upsetting and stressful, and worse was to come. We had heard nothing about the glands test, so I rang again and was told the result was negative! So she had not had TB after all, and we had lost our best cow, who gave eight gallons of milk a day at her peak. Our vet told us later that the method of testing had been changed and that other farmers had suffered similarly. We eventually received a clearance form.

We had other problems during these weeks, although they seemed minor in comparison. Sally had ringworm, requiring treatment. A lamb injured her hind leg jumping over a fence and had it in plaster for three weeks. Shandy started limping and keeping one leg off the ground. The vet said he had a temperature and prescribed antibiotics for four days. Judy, our Guernsey cow, became very poorly with acetonaemia and was almost blind. An injection hadn't cured her, so we were given two bottles of green drench to try. We gave her one in the afternoon and in the evening she was in the field fighting three Friesians! John and I felt like trying the other bottle to get us fighting fit, as I had just recovered from flu and was now starting a heavy cold, and John's back was being very troublesome, and also he had just broken his reading glasses.

One day we had bullocks in Lane Field with our cows and they had obviously been fighting, as one of Betsy's horns was bleeding. There was also blood in her milk from an injured quarter. The same day we had sheep in the mowing grass at Collins. We had such a small acreage, but it was a magnet for other farmers' stock. At least we didn't have this trouble from Sam.

We were haymaking in five fields during the first half of June, and the weather let us down. It drizzled on and off throughout, but we baled it all on the better days. Our friends, Joy, Fred and family, came as usual to carry in the bales. We had two haymaking machines break down. As soon as we finished we had two weeks of dry and very hot weather with record temperatures being broken daily! Of course, the grass, which was badly needed for the cows, didn't grow in the cut fields.

Fortunately, on 4th July, we had a terrific thunderstorm with torrential rain and hailstones. Lightning kept striking the stones outside the garden gate. The rain brought mud and gravel down the lane and into the shippen and dairy, so we had to shovel it out and wash down. The electricity was off for several hours, and milking was not finished until eleven thirty.

Next day we enjoyed good baths, with plenty of water for a change. We also started cleaning the shippen walls and floor, using lashings of water. A further thunderstorm on the 7th kept the well topped up.

For better news, Maggie and family had come to stay at Easter and for the spring Bank Holiday week, which helped to lighten the gloom. John was always up for milking at five thirty, and however quietly he sneaked downstairs so as not to disturb anybody, Michael always heard him and followed down. He loved to 'help' Granddad with the milking, and I don't think he ever missed while he was with us – even on cold, wet mornings.

Maggie brought overcoats and other clothing items and she, and a kind lady from Portishead, frequently picked up bargains from jumble sales for us. It saved us from wearing our best clothes for work, and we were very grateful.

For some time we had been keen to try making cheese, but had been unable to find a suitable cheese press. When we saw an advertisement that someone near Exeter was making these, we rang them straightaway. Within two days Rodney Wheeler and his mother brought a press for our inspection, and we were so impressed that we bought it for £26. They were such pleasant, friendly people who were most interested in our venture and invited us to visit them in their smallholding. We became good friends with them.

I couldn't wait to try out the cheese making, and I was totally absorbed with it. It turned out to be very successful. Luckily we still had two Ayrshire cows, as their milk was said to be the most suitable. As a child I used to wonder about Miss Muffet eating her curds and whey. At last I have discovered what curds and whey are, and it is extremely unlikely that anyone could contemplate eating them!

The little cheeses looked so attractive, wrapped in muslin and standing on the larder shelf. We had to wait for some weeks for them to mature; the longer they stood the better the flavour. Unfortunately I didn't realise that the temperature in the larder had to be just right, and as it fluctuated considerably throughout the year some of the cheeses were spoilt.

On 8th July we went to a buffet luncheon at the manor. It was a sumptuous spread attended by eighty-three people, all by invitation. We thoroughly enjoyed it.

Soon after we had the thunderstorms in July, Aunty Edie came to stay again. We had just discovered our wash-up trough was leaking badly, and John had to buy a new one quickly for washing the milking equipment. He then fixed washers over the holes in the old one, put in plenty of water and sheep dip, and Aunty and I helped him to dip our lambs. It was some job! They were being troubled with maggots in this humid weather. They seemed to know we were helping them, as they were very brave and certainly much happier afterwards.

The recent weather had resulted in a fine crop of

mushrooms again, and Aunty was delighted to be here to gather them, as she did last year. She was with us for twenty-six days this time. John took her home, but the clutch went on the car at Newton Poppleford and they had to wait at a garage until four fifteen before it was replaced. John was home just before nine, when we had to milk, clear up, feed calves etc. It was a very hot day and I had done a big wash and ironed it all, and also cleaned through the house, so we had both found it a very tiring day. At least Aunty paid the garage bill – about £45

August started off dry. The grass was not growing and we were having to feed the cows rolled oats and concentrates. John was now taking water to Collins as the stream had dried up. We were told that someone further along was damming it to keep water for their own stock. We had very hot, dry days from 4th to 29th August, which meant constant trips to the river and it was often taking five hours a day. The milk was dropping, as there was only a little dry grass for the cows.

We collected Michael and Catherine on 12th August to stay with us on their own. Catherine was just getting over mumps and was a bit niggly in the hot weather. A few days later she lost her appetite and was running a temperature. I rang the doctor, who promised to call that evening. I kept her in bed and by the time he came she was much better and demanding sausage and baked beans! A compete recovery.

When Maggie and Iain came on 26th they brought fifteen gallons of water, which helped in the house. They also encouraged the rain, as usual, because on the 29th we had another torrential thunderstorm. How we welcomed this!

In early September we visited the Wheeler family –

Greta, Geoff and Rodney. They were very welcoming and we enjoyed an interesting evening, finishing with a good supper. Greta gave us rennet, starter (for the cheese making), her homemade sausages and tomato ketchup to take home. She also told us of a water diviner who had found them plenty of water.

We rang the diviner, Arthur Salter of Luppit, near Honiton, and he promised to come to us, and to David, to try to find us water. It was so exciting to see him walking around the fields, especially when he announced he had found water at twenty feet, near the caravan. It was an ideal position to bring water down to the house. We rang a firm re. digging in preparation for sinking a well. We also contacted the Ministry of Agriculture, who said we must get written permission for a well in advance, and they sent us an application form for a grant. At this time many homes in north and mid Devon were using standpipes, their mains water having been cut off due to the severe drought.

A week after 'finding' the water, the digger was set to work and we watched excitedly as it went lower and lower into the ground. At twenty feet it was still completely dry. They tried a few more feet, but it was still as dry as dust! A bitter disappointment. Mr Salter came the next day, very apologetic, and explained that he was deceived by a mineral seam of iron oxide which gave him the same reaction as water. It was the same for David. Fortunately we had a fair amount of rain after this, including another thunderstorm, and this rain continued throughout October, so we were all right for a few months.

A sad day for us in early November when Betsy calved in the meadow, but her Charolais X bull calf was dead.

We had intended rearing it. Other calves had been arriving without problems, and those we sent to market were fetching better prices again.

December was a cold month and fairly uneventful until the 19th when we went to Maggie's for the day. It meant John having to get up at four thirty for milking and me at six thirty. Nan, John's mother, came and Iain's father came in the afternoon. John's parents had separated some years ago, and his mother had not felt able to make the long and awkward journey to Kinnings. However, we wrote to each other frequently, and it was nice to see her for a good chat.

On Christmas Day we rang Maggie as usual and spoke to the children. In the evening we went to the Hernimans. It was an enjoyable visit and we stayed late. Our family turned up on the 31st, and that ended 1976.

Chapter VII

1977

On 1st January the meet for the Tiverton staghounds was at Leslie Baker's farm. John and the family went up. It was cold, wet and windy, but Michael and Catherine were given a sausage roll and a sandwich, which cheered them up.

Next day, Fred, Joy and Stephen came. We had a jolly evening. Catherine was very taken with Stephen, who was about fifteen, and announced she was going to marry him. Maggie came to his rescue and had a game of 'Master Mind' with him.

We had snow showers on four days in January, but luckily it didn't pitch. One day we saw eleven partridges in our field for the first time. We often get pheasants – especially the colourful cock birds. Once John caught one eating rolled oats in the shippen and brought him up to the house. 'What shall I do with him?' he asked me.

We were both partial to a pheasant dinner, but as I looked at him, so frightened and helpless, I couldn't contemplate eating him. 'Let him go,' I said. He was off in a flash, and we didn't see him again!

In February we bought two good heifers from Fred and Joy and they bought two of our calves. At the same time Judy had to be sent barren when her udder shrivelled up. She had been poorly on and off for some time.

We were very busy throughout February cleaning calf

houses and the old shippen. On dry days John was busy clearing the orchard in readiness for vegetables, and we were both repairing hedges at Collins. I planted shallots and broad beans in the garden, but the pheasants ate my beans. Next time we catch a pheasant he's for the oven!

We had made up our minds not to rear tame lambs this year, but suddenly decided on two at Barnstaple market. There were forty there altogether, all looking so sweet it was difficult to resist them. We bought two lively little ones; Percy for £6.50, and Polly for £8. John ringed their tails after a few days, which would cause them to drop off later, and also castrated Percy. 'Ow!' he yelled, and looked quite miserable for a while. Polly was terribly concerned about him, and kept running after us to tell us about him, or was it to tell us off? We fenced around part of the front garden for them, but Percy always managed to get out. Then Polly would come to the front door baaing loudly to let us know so that we could find him and re-unite them. These two were the most entertaining lambs that we had reared, and I'm afraid we spoilt them. However, it paid off as they did very well and quickly put on weight.

As we were not using the caravan these days we wired off the patch of ground around it, opened the door of the toilet compartment (which was empty) and put in some hay and nuts and a container of water outside. It made a nice shelter and sleeping quarters for them. Two men from the post office came to creosote the telegraph pole which stood in their patch, and remarked what lucky lambs they were to have their own caravan!

When they were bigger and out in the field they let the children sit on them. Percy even gave Michael a short ride. There were blackberries in the hedges in Hill Field and one day when we were picking them the lambs joined in and discovered these were something tasty to eat. They were crafty enough to go ahead of us, biting off any easily reachable fruit. If the berries weren't ripe enough, they spat them out! We were quite amazed at this behaviour and moved them elsewhere for fear of any ill effects.

I felt very sad when it was time for John to take them to the abattoir, as they had become real pets in their six months with us. Nevertheless, we had Percy back for the freezer. We had a nasty shock when a separate bag came with his carcass, containing his head still with wool on! John quickly buried it in the orchard. This had never happened with previous lambs, and we found it very upsetting.

Our haymaking this year took place during June and July in rather unsettled weather. This was obvious by the fact that John's first visit to the river for water was on 31st July.

John noticed one day that Henrietta had a swollen knee. When it didn't improve he consulted the vet who, after examination, announced she had housemaid's knee, for which there is no cure! We realised what had probably caused this: whenever John let the cows into their new strip of fresh grass, Henrietta always went towards the following strip, knelt down by the fence, pushed her head forward and started on that. So while the rest of the cows were happy to start on the new grass, Henrietta could be seen on her knees snatching at the next section. This may well have caused the swelling.

We decided to give up milk within the next year. Our churns were often collected late nowadays, which meant they were left on the stand for hours in the hot sun. Also we had heard that churn collection was to cease later on, and that the milk would be collected in bulk tanks. As our lane, from the entrance to the dairy, was almost half a mile and very steep and stony, bulk tanks would be useless for us. There would be an incentive for going out of milk, as it was decided that too much was being produced. We would have to send our cows as barreners, which was not a happy thought, but unfortunately we had no alternative.

We were seeing the Wheeler family quite frequently during 1977. On one occasion we arranged to buy half a pig from them. We collected it one evening and were persuaded to stay for supper – not that we needed much persuasion, as Greta always provided lovely homemade delicacies. We arrived home as twelve forty and still had to sort out the meat for the freezer! Next day we managed to get some saltpetre (potassium nitrate) from the vet for pickling the pork, and we put two half hams, a piece of belly (for bacon) and the trotters into buckets. The result was excellent and it all tasted delicious.

This was the year when a British girl, Virginia Wade, won the ladies final at Wimbledon, which was very exciting.

On 4th August we fetched the children from Nailsea. We had warm, sunny weather for two weeks, so we were able to have a picnic on Instow beach one day, and in Rock Park, Barnstaple, the following week. We also had campfires by the caravan on Saturday evenings with their favourite bangers and beans. On the third Saturday Maggie and Iain arrived and we decided on another campfire. We should have known better, because halfway through the heavens opened and John had to get the car to take us down to the house. In the ten days they were here they only had four dry days – the other six were with rain and even a thunderstorm. They are definitely rainmakers!

In September we were delighted to be visited by Joyce, an old school friend, and her husband Alec. As they are both doctors living in Nottingham, a visit had seemed unlikely, but they were spending their holiday in Dulverton with their caravan – a comparatively short distance away. They helped us sample Percy's leg with veg, apple tart and cream and cheese and biscuits. On Sunday we had tea in their caravan and found plenty to talk about. It was an enjoyable change for us.

In October John went to the first session of a calf-rearing course, which involved a different visit to a farm each week. He picked up interesting information on these courses, and all the latest methods.

We had had eleven cows calving since August, and apart from Clementine's, which was stillborn, all went well. Betsy was the last to calve this year, and this time she had just what we wanted – a nice Limousin X Jersey bull calf. She was very proud of him.

The rest of the year proceeded fairly uneventfully. We had some strong gales during November, which blew our new fowl house away. John had to catch the birds and put them back in their old house until he could fix stakes to firm down the new one.

We had more strong winds in December, and force ten gales on the 23rd. I had a busy day cleaning through the house ready for Christmas. The wet and mud from the recent rain had taken its toll on our floors, and I went to bed well satisfied that all looked very clean again.

At about twelve thirty we were awakened by a deafening bang. 'Whatever was that?' I asked. We listened for a few moments but heard nothing further.

Reluctantly John struggled out of bed. 'I suppose I'd better have a look.' It was lucky he did. He was back very quickly. 'It looks as if the roof's off the lambs' shed. I'll have to dress and get out there.' I followed him down.

The electricity was off and we were groping around for torches. From the back door we could see that the roof of the outbuildings had come off, which included the old shippen, calf and pig houses and two store sheds. Fortunately there were no livestock housed there at the time. The roof consisted of several galvanised panels, all fixed together, and much of this had finished up in Well Field, which was amazing considering the weight of it. One portion had landed on the roof of our house. Electric cables were lying in the passageway between the house and the outbuildings, and sparks were flashing and cracking in the darkness. It was a terrifying scene.

John rang 999. The police said that as the fireman were on strike a policeman would have to come first to see if it was necessary to call out part-timers who were covering for emergencies. When he arrived he took one look and phoned for them immediately. He said we were a number one priority as a fire hazard.

Eventually the fire engine trundled down the lane with lights flashing. John also phoned the emergency number for SWEB, explaining the cable situation and they sent out three men. There were twelve men here altogether, including John, all with torches coming through the front door, through the kitchen and out through the back door. It was a nightmare situation, which seemed to go on for hours, and I couldn't help thinking of all the dirt being tracked through after my hard work cleaning the day before!

I managed to make tea for everyone by heating water

on the Rayburn – although it was a job to find enough cups and mugs in the dark! It seemed the night would never end, but finally the power was restored – mainly to enable John to milk, and it was considered safe enough to leave us. It was almost five o'clock when they all went. John decided to milk the cows then rather than go back to bed, but I managed two hours' sleep.

John fetched Fred and the boys mid-morning to help him cover the contents of the outhouse with heavy polythene sheeting. He had already contacted the local builder for urgent repairs to the house roof, but the whole firm had just broken up for two weeks' holiday! Fortunately the boss's nephew turned up and stayed until late evening doing temporary repairs to the slates and guttering in order to keep out the rain. It was certainly some whirlwind that hit us, and it would be a long time before all the damage was repaired.

Joy kindly invited us for Christmas dinner, but we had prepared our own so we went to her for the evening instead. Our neighbours had heard nothing throughout the night, and it was only when Mr Wright looked across from the chalet that he came over to investigate. He told us that the outbuildings had been thatched until around 1929 when they were replaced by the galvanised roof – probably the same time that the house thatch was replaced with slates.

We had a pleasanter kind of excitement on the 27th when we collected a border collie puppy. I had been nervous of dogs since as a child I had been badly bitten by one, but had to agree reluctantly that it was a necessity for sheep. I soon fell in love with this pretty little 'Lassie'-type creature, who was shivering and nervous of us when parted from her mother. She was sick twice and messed in the car coming home, but apart from crying occasionally she soon recovered. She loved her bed in the wooden hut, which had once housed the loo before the farmhouse was modernised. We called her Bess and she became a favourite with the children when our family came for the New Year. On 31st December, a mild, sunny day, Iain took the roofing sections to pieces and sorted them out. He also repaired the mower. There were always plenty of jobs awaiting his attention!

Chapter VIII
1978

Throughout January the weather changed from day to day: dry and mild one day, then rain, gales, sunny and warm, hailstones, thunder, cold with snow storms and finally frost and fog. On the 29th we had terrible gales throughout the night and all the following day. We had a sleepless night and discovered slates off the roof again, but John was unable to get a ladder up because of the strong winds. The Rayburn was smoking so badly we had to put it out. On the 31st there were more flashes and bangs and John spent a long time repairing wires. We kept ringing the builder but nobody came to us.

On fine days I was taking Bess for short walks. She was very excitable and kept biting my legs – not serious biting, just nipping, but I found it very off-putting.

However, it was good to receive approval for going out of milk from the Ministry of Agriculture, as well as identity cards for our cows. We then joined the North Devon Meat Company and invested £100. They would be taking the cows, in batches, for slaughter.

We started buying tame lambs and finished up with twenty-three. We always gave them names, and two amusing ones this year were Jeeves and Bertie Wooster. Then there was Sylvester. I mistakenly bought him as a ewe lamb only to discover that he was a little ram. He appeared to be almost pure Suffolk, so we decided to keep him as our ram.

On 8th February, the carpenter and mate started work on the roof of the stores – at last! It was such a relief to us. They came again next day, worked well, and finished the job.

A couple of days later there was a very heavy frost. The taps were frozen in the dairy and there was no water reaching the dairy tank until mid-afternoon. John had to fill churns from the house for the cows. By teatime there was no water coming through at all, although the well was full. I rang the plumber and John collected two churns of water from Presbury. Aside from this, the tractor had packed up at the top of our lane when John was taking up the milk. Also, one of the small lambs was limping and needed tablets and penicillin, as well as powder puffed into a runny eye. We always kept plenty of medications handy for these tame lambs as they frequently had problems.

The plumber came very early the next day and replaced a valve in the well, but it needed a new strainer which he would fit later. We then discovered that the hot water was not coming through the taps, so John put an electric fire in the loft. It was snowing in the evening. I was feeling very tired and fed up, but worse was yet to come…

Next day there was very heavy frost again on top of the snow. Neither tractor would start. Murch's man came to see to the one in the lane. The milk lorry couldn't get up Presbury Hill to collect our churns, so David brought up his small tractor to collect them, but his gave up as well! Fortunately most of the snow thawed later and it was all collected from the stand the following day. The North Devon Meat Company came to collect our first three cows, but we had to drive them up the lane to the cattle truck.

It was very cold on the 15th, with easterly winds. We had rain in the afternoon, which turned to snow in the evening. The electricity went off at five past nine and when we took the bottles of milk across to the lambs by torchlight at ten o'clock, we were surprised to be struggling through deep snow. At least we had had a letter that day to say that our insurance claims for the whirlwind damage would be met in full.

There was plenty of snow on the ground the next day, and further falls later. The electric was off all day and John did not milk at all, although the cows were mooing. The following day was the same: everything white and no electric. John started milking by hand, and Melanie had almost filled a plastic bucket when she kicked it all over John and split the bucket, so he gave up. We rang SWEB again, who told us our transformer was faulty and had to be replaced. We were reconnected at noon after thirty-nine hours without electric. John was then able to milk the cows by machine and the pump was working again to bring water from the well.

On the 18th the lying snow was frozen and there was a further heavy fall with gale-force easterly winds: no milk collection today. We woke on the 19th to find there had been heavy snow during the night, and this restarted at midday, still with gale-force winds. Every road in North Devon was impassable in the morning. Many were without power or water, but we were okay this time, as the transformer had been replaced just in time. There was snow in the cubicle house and the calf and lamb houses.

Maurice rang about his fifteen bullocks in the field adjoining ours. These were the wretched creatures that kept getting through and upsetting our cows, but John took them hay and straw for eight days until Maurice could get to them again. On the 21st John managed to get the tractor up our lane, as he needed bags of feed. I walked up in the tractor tracks and was amazed at the sight beyond our gate. The road was packed solid with frozen snow despite the fact that we were now having a slight thaw and a little rain; it had no effect here. The four churns on the stand were completely covered, as were the hedges. One man from the village was actually walking along the top of the hedge! Until I saw this, I had not realised we were trapped.

We were advised to let the cows drink the milk, as it was said that one gallon of milk was equal to 1½ lbs of cake. John poured some into their water trough, but on sampling it they turned away in disgust!

The main road below Presbury had now been cleared and the snow in the fields was thawing as it became milder and there was a little rain each day. Our road remained blocked. There were now certain collection points for churns on the main roads, and John managed to get some through the fields, but it was very hit and miss.

On the 23rd we heard on the radio that minor roads were being left to clear themselves. I was furious and rang the council, but of course they denied this.

On the 25th we heard that the snowplough had cleared part of our road from the village but had stopped well short of us. Maurice rang to say that he would arrange snow clearance the next day. His bulldozer arrived and cleared as far as our gate and then broke down! It was finally cleared on the 27th, so we were now quite free for the tractor and car. Unfortunately the milk lorry could still not reach us; there was not sufficient room for it on our narrow road with snow banked up on each side. We were having heavy rain each day and the fields were saturated.

On 2nd March the milk lorry collected from our stand at last – the first time for fifteen days. Lorna calved safely and Jenny calved the next day, both with bull calves.

We had ordered some calf pens several weeks before the bad weather, but were having trouble getting them delivered. They were always being promised, but never arrived. I finally lost patience and rang National Carriers three times on 9th March, and eventually the deputy manager brought them at six o'clock.

On 23rd March Dinah calved at ten thirty, so we were late getting to bed. Next morning (Good Friday) we discovered our bigger lambs were missing and decided they were lost in the woods. Samantha, on her pony, and Christopher with two puppies, helped us catch them. It was quite a performance. Then the chain broke on the dung spreader and Princess decided to calve at dinnertime. We were exhausted by the time the family arrived at teatime. It was wet most of the weekend for them, but Maggie cleaned out the store for us.

In April we decided to change our car again. We chose a Renault 16 and had a good allowance on our estate. We found the Renault very comfortable to ride in.

We bought a collar and lead for Bess, but when we tried her on the lead she howled and cried like a baby. However, a couple of days later we took her to Collins to collect the cows, and she was quite well behaved.

On 8th May the builder sent four men to work all day and three men again the next morning. The following day the electricians turned up. Two weeks later the mason and two others stayed all day, and at last the work was finished, after five months!

After shopping in South Molton one Thursday we arrived home to find sixteen of Maurice's bullocks in our orchard. They had trampled over our vegetable patch and eaten at least a dozen cabbages. We drove them up the lane with the help of Bess. At only seven months she proved to be good with cattle, and although one bullock kicked her in the face she stuck doggedly to her task. Maurice came over in the evening and he and John had another go at improving the hedge in the meadow.

We did have one amusing incident for a change – at least, I found it amusing. We were trying to get four calves down to the meadow and they were being very stubborn and difficult. Eventually two of them went in the right direction, but Florence and William decided to jump into the slurry pit. John managed to pull Florence out, but in reaching for William he fell in himself! I had to help pull him out, which was some job as I was doubled up with laughter. He emerged minus his wellies, with his clothes stinking and filthy up to the waist. I insisted he stood on the doorstep and took everything off before he entered the house. It really was hilarious, but he couldn't see the joke!

We started haymaking on June 12th. Guy cut the grass in Hill Field at eight o'clock. Apart from a tyre bursting on the hay turner and rain on the third day, it went smoothly and it was finally baled on the 18th – 443 bales of the best hay we had ever made. I stacked the bales and John carried them all in himself over two days.

Now the bad news! Our milk was not collected as the lorry drivers were on strike. We found it on the stand the next morning quite sour. I used some to make five batches of scones, which accounted for 1½ pints from 26 gallons! The next day's milk was wasted too. Then we heard that we could leave churns in South Molton market, which John did for two days, by which time the strike was over.

Our second haymaking in three fields at Collins did not go so well, as it rained day after day, but it was baled eventually. Chris Herniman, who was on holiday, helped John carry in most of the bales, and Iain helped with the rest at the weekend.

It was discovered that weekend that Catherine had German measles so had to stay here for the week. Poor Michael was bitterly disappointed, but had to return to school.

30th June was our last day for sending milk to the dairy, which meant that I was about to start cream, butter and cheese making once more until the remainder of our cows went for slaughter.

July was fairly uneventful until the 30th when Gwyneth rang with the sad news that Will, my old boss, had died. We had so enjoyed their visits to us. I wrote to her, promising to call on her next Sunday on our way to Maggie's.

Next day North Devon Meat Company collected five more cows, which made eleven gone. We felt rather sad at losing our cows, but weather problems and strikes had made milking difficult. We were hoping for easier times now... I wonder?

We visited Gwyneth, as promised, went to Maggie's for dinner and brought the children back for their summer holidays. They helped us creosote buildings, clear weeds and light bonfires. We had campfires and visits to Instow beach and Rock Park, Barnstaple, for picnics. We collected two little weaner pigs from Denzil's son, Ian, and two more just four days later.

On Saturday we went to the Chittlehamholt Revel in

aid of the new village hall. There was a gymkhana, six-aside football, clay shooting and hot air ballooning, and the children enjoyed races and pony rides. A most enjoyable day.

On 18th August we received our first compensation cheque for going out of milk. We were to receive £8,000 altogether, and this would come in stages to enable us to build up alternative livestock. Maggie and Iain turned up in the evening.

Ruth calved the next day. Iain started building a wall in the pigsty, which had almost collapsed. It was to make two separate sections, and he made a very good job of it. The weaners were very happy and doing well. We also bought a dozen pullets to keep the egg supply going.

We received £13 in wool money for our first lambs. Fred had sheared fifteen for us and John managed three. I thought his looked rather strange, but it was his first attempt as he unfortunately missed his instruction week when doing the sheep course. The lambs were later collected by Clifford Ley for dipping so they wouldn't be troubled by maggots.

Sally was the next to calve, followed soon after by Lulu. John had left home early to fetch Aunty Edie with instructions for me to keep an eye on Lulu. I could see her by the hedge looking as if calving was imminent, but nothing arrived. By mid afternoon I was rather anxious and rang David. He and Denzil turned up and decided the calf had to be pulled off. They wanted her in the shippen and I was able to lead her in quite easily. John arrived just as her bull calf was delivered.

In September John relief-milked for Brian Waldron for a week. Denzil had suggested he would pay him for doing this while Brian and family had a holiday. Later he was to milk two days a month for him.

John was busy fixing the new calf pens in the cubicle house, and a dealer was getting calves for us from Taunton and Exeter markets. Denzil obtained ten ewe lambs for us at Bideford – Hampshire Down X Masham. He and Beryl delivered them to us. This made twenty-four in all, plus Sylvester.

We had ordered ten strong wooden gates for Kinnings and Collins to replace the poor ones, and John started hanging these and checking the hedges in readiness for the sheep. We injected the twenty-four lambs with Covexin, gave the new ten a worm drench and trimmed all their feet. When Margaret and Dorothy came a couple of days later, they helped us to take them along the road to Collins.

In October the Devon and Somerset staghounds were on the road when we went to fetch our cows. They acted like maniacs, bursting through hedges and frightening livestock in the fields. Twinkle, the little pony, was so scared that he ran off, but John was eventually able to catch him for Rosalyn. Our cows always gave very little milk when the hunt was around.

Maggie rang on 28th October to say that Michael and Catherine had received badges for swimming 200 metres – great news!

Earlier in the month John had spent a day helping David to pick apples from his orchard. He brought home about two cwt, so I had to get busy, sorting and dealing with them. I made two lots of cider, apple jelly, apple chutney, blackberry and apple jam and froze apple pulp ready for pies.

On 30th October we put a harness on Sylvester, complete with green wax crayon, and took him along to Collins in our new trailer. The ewes rushed forward to greet him, and we left him surrounded by them. He had grown into a fine looking ram. We walked along to see them next morning and were pleasantly surprised to find three green bottoms already. There were thirteen marked in two weeks. We changed to a red crayon and after a further two weeks to a blue crayon. After six weeks all but three were marked and we took off Sylvester's harness.

October had been a very dry month throughout. The family came on the 20th and brought containers of water with them. They didn't bring rain this time, just a little drizzle. We had ten gallons of water from Denzil. We had also been fetching water from Brian, for baths, as we didn't fancy washing ourselves in river water with the river so low. Denzil and Brian were both fortunate enough to have mains water. It was 12th November before we had any significant rain.

There was a bread strike in November. I made four loaves in case it lasted. Luckily it was short lived, as I had plenty of work without bread making!

Sam rang to suggest we shared ten tons of feed potatoes with him. These would cost only £14 a ton and would be stained with purple to ensure they would not be used for human consumption. It turned out to be a good idea. The cattle loved them cut up raw; the pigs and hens needed theirs boiled. These were best quality potatoes, but there was a surplus this year, hence the offer by the Potato Marketing Board. The purple was on the skins only and had not penetrated to the insides. We found them good enough to eat!

We picked bucketfuls of mushrooms in the meadow, which was amazing for November, but was owing to the warm, sunny weather in October followed by the recent rain.

On 29th November the lorry came for our six remaining cows. They were rather difficult to load, except for Betsy, who climbed up without fuss. She was our very first cow and I shed a tear, for we had become very fond of her. We had only four cows to milk now: those that had calved in August and September. John preferred to milk them and feed the milk to the calves in buckets.

We had a side of beef back from North Devon Meat Company. It was from Isabel II, a young cow, and was very tender and had a delicious flavour.

We had a phone call to say that two dogs were worrying our sheep at Collins. John hurried along there with his gun, but when he recognised the dogs he didn't shoot, just scared them away. We didn't want trouble with a neighbour, but of course John had a few strong words with him. We just hoped it wouldn't happen again as they were biting the sheep and there was wool everywhere.

The family came to us on 22nd December for two days. We had a Christmas dinner on the 23rd – a Wyandotte which John had caponised. It was a super bird, weighing almost 9 lbs. We tried our homemade cider and blackberry wine. When they went home the following afternoon we went to Uncle Ken's, had a good meal and caught up on the latest news.

On Boxing Day John killed two cockerels and we plucked them for the freezer and I made white bread. Recently I had made three brown loaves, as I had to use up all the strong flour I had bought during the bread strike. It really was delicious with our own butter, cheese and ham, so I thought I might continue making bread for a while. I did begrudge spending so long in the kitchen, though, cooking and baking, and much preferred to be working outside, even mucking out!

On the 28th we bought two heifer calves at South Molton market and a further one from Denzil. We collected his and had tea and Christmas cake with him and Beryl.

On the 31st everywhere was white with snow and it was freezing. Many roads were impassable in North Devon – including ours, of course – and also the Barnstaple to Exeter road. We managed to move our bullocks back from Collins and later the sheep through a narrow passageway, assisted by Rosalyn and her Jack Russell. What an end to the year!

Chapter IX
1979

January 1979 began with snow and ice. Water was frozen in the hot tap in the bathroom and in the cold tap in the kitchen all day, as well as in the dairy. We collected buckets and containers of water from the bath tap. Diesel froze in the tractor. John put two oil heaters upstairs and an electric fire in the loft! Next day no water came into the tank from the well until evening.

Heavy snow had been forecast, so John took the tractor and link box to South Molton to collect animal feed, paraffin and veterinary supplies. He helped two motorists who were stuck along the icy road. Luckily the snow bypassed the southwest this time, but it was still freezing. The cows were slipping down outside the shippen and were reluctant to walk there.

John started a beef course, which involved a visit to an abattoir once a week. There were six weekly sessions, but he was forced to miss one because of further snow and ice. He did, however, manage to get to David's where he had started occasional milking in addition to milking for Brian every other Sunday. John had also enquired about milk recording for the Milk Marketing Board as another means of income. This involved going to a dairy farm at a morning and afternoon milking once a month and recording the milk given by each cow and the total amount of milk in the bulk tank. He was also to take a sample from each cow in a little bottle and check the individual quality, such as butterfat content. A sample was also taken from the bulk tank. If the farmers required this service they were charged for it, but the recorder was paid by the MMB according to the number of cows he had recorded. John signed for this on 15th January and soon had two or three farms on his list in addition to occasional relief recording.

Bess was taken to be spayed, which was a relief as Rosalyn's dog Dan had been worrying her recently. The day she was due to have the stitches out it snowed again, so that visit was delayed. When John took her eventually she cried the whole time. She's a terrible baby!

In February there were sheep scab cases reported and a compulsory dipping order came in. This meant there were hardly any tame lambs coming onto the market. We had bought only two so far and were hoping to get more settled in before our own were born. We started enquiring from neighbours and farms round about and finally ended up with thirteen. I missed choosing and bidding for them at the market and seeing the friends we had made there.

March was a mainly cold, wet month with just the odd warm day. We found traces of mice in the lamb shed so we set two traps. We caught four mice, one small rat and Bess's nose in five days! Bess was not hurt, just shocked.

The big event was on the 27th. Our own first lamb arrived; a ewe lamb, quite strong. We had the expectant mums in the centre of the cubicle house where we could inspect them easily. They all lambed on their own, which was a relief to us. In fact it was a surprise as these were their first lambs. Two of them were awkward and not interested in their offspring, so we had to deal with these.

This may have been the reason why another lambed, unexpectedly, one night and we found her with two dead lambs. She was quite unconcerned. On the whole we were well pleased with the good lambs produced and with Sylvester, our ram.

3rd May was polling day for the general and local elections. Next day we learned that the Conservatives were to form the new government, with Margaret Thatcher as our first woman Prime Minister – an exciting change! We visited Uncle Ken in the evening and he was moaning at having a woman in charge, but as time went by he changed his mind.

One morning, when we were gathering our lambs together for an inspection, we noticed one against the hedge, looking very miserable. I picked him up to carry him into the warm kitchen, followed by Sylvester who kept pushing me and being altogether unpleasant. Obviously he objected to my taking the lamb away, and from that day on he butted me on every possible occasion. He would stand back and then charge at me, bruising my hands which I put forward in self-defence. I just couldn't believe it was the same animal I had bottle fed and fussed over! I was very nervous of this feisty ram and kept out of his way. He also went for Maggie and Rosalyn, but was quite friendly with the men and with Michael.

Several lambs had been scouring quite badly and the sample showed they had coccidiosis. What with this and orf it was a pleasant relief to send seven healthy young bullocks of twelve to sixteen months to the South Molton special stores sale. They fetched £1,360. Later on we sold a further eight for £1,659.

North Devon Meat Company collected our three

young cows, who were now dry, leaving Lulu behind as a house cow. I was still making cheese and butter.

June started and Brian sheared our sheep. Next day we had all the sheep and lambs in for a drench and sprayed them against flies. We had to house the hens as the crows, or magpies, were pinching their eggs. John Dennis rang to offer John two relief recordings but, much as he would have appreciated the extra money, he could only manage one.

Haymaking time was coming around again, so the hay grass was rolled, thistles and docks cleared, and there was plenty to do in the garden as well. I helped outside as much as possible. Then Denzil rang, needing help with his silage. John did fourteen hours for him over four days.

Eileen Parsons called in one day and noticed our gooseberry bushes had been completely stripped by sawfly. She rang later to say she had gooseberries to spare and would leave some in the shed by our entrance. We were surprised to find almost 9 lbs there, so I made 12 lbs of jam and put the rest in the freezer. We were even more surprised to find a further 9 lbs there a few days later! We gave her some cream and cheese in return. Eileen has been a favourite of mine since she thought Michael and Catherine were our children and was genuinely surprised on being told they were our grandchildren!

On 26th June John cut Hill Field in the morning and afternoon and the top of Lane Field in the evening. Three days later David cut our grass at Collins and John milked for him twice in lieu of payment. We had 1,040 bales of very good hay.

In July David and his father inspected our bullocks

and bought a Hereford steer and Devon steer for £230 each. We sold six more at Barnstaple later.

It was about time we had another calamity in the house and right on cue water started dripping through above the kitchen doorway. We went upstairs and discovered it was coming from the tank in the airing cupboard. Everything in there was soaking wet. We phoned for Mr Boucher – how fortunate we were to have found such a reliable plumber! He came the next morning and fitted a new cylinder. He seemed fascinated with our misfortunes and each time he came he told me I should write my memoirs to recoup the expenses. There was no chance of that – it was as much as I could do to keep up a correspondence with relations and friends...

That summer we picked 24 lbs of blackcurrants and raspberries (which the birds shared with us), and were given strawberries as well as the gooseberries. This resulted in plenty of jam making. Later on we had several pounds of runner beans given to us, which meant I had to prepare and freeze these. No escape from the kitchen!

John started burning the old paint off the front windowpanes. He discovered the kitchen one was quite rotten so ordered a new frame from South Molton, which was to take at least a week. We fixed large polythene bags in the window space and were busy with this when, to our amazement, a Walls' ice cream van passed the house and drove down to the shippen playing the usual jingle! Goodness knows why he came down our long, stony lane, as he didn't call anywhere else. Anyway, we always kept plenty of ice cream in the freezer, so we just waved him away.

A week later we collected the window casement and John spent most of the day fitting it. It was a nice change to go to Presbury in the evening, picking peas that they offered us, and then going into the house for a chat with Beth.

Now it was time for the feisty Sylvester to start earning his living again. On went his harness and crayon and he joined his ladies. He was welcomed enthusiastically. He was very popular, and he knew it. They were soon being regularly marked, as they had been the year before.

On 5th August we fetched Michael and Catherine, who were useful, as usual. They helped us get Tim back from another farm, where he had been hobnobbing with some Jersey heifers for a few days. There was plenty of chasing about before he returned.

We were waiting for Lulu to calve and she started at breakfast time on the 14th. The children went up in the field with John. Suddenly Catherine rushed into the kitchen, so excited she could hardly speak. 'It's two,' she was saying, 'It's two, Gran!'

I just couldn't believe she meant two calves, but I hurried with her to find out. And there they were, two healthy bull calves with Lulu fussing over them. One was bigger than the other, so we called them Little and Large.

Maggie and Iain turned up for tea on the 17th and found us busy as usual, as John had painted the window frames and now had started putting Sandtex on the outside walls. Maurice's heifer was here again, and we kept her shut in until he collected her. John took five of our lambs to North Devon Meat Company. Bill Ward, an old friend from Bristol, was staying at Croyde so visited us with Rose and their two grandsons. Two of our bullocks were missing. They had gone into Mr Hipkiss's garden! Rosalyn rang for John's help with a calving. A good Charolais bull calf arrived safely.

On the 20th we had a call to say that Hetty had died, so I immediately wrote a letter of sympathy to Eric, her son. On the 21st we collected two weaners from Brian. With relief milking, recording, gardening, cooking etc. there were never enough hours in a day. All the family returned on 27th August.

Brian went on holiday for a week on 1st September, so John milked his cows. He also fed his pigs, hens, cats, dog and goldfish. Quite a job!

On 4th September the children rang us. Michael had swum two miles and earned a long distance badge and Catherine had swum one mile. Wonderful news!

Little and Large had grown very well in four weeks, having been left with Lulu, but we then took them to South Molton market. They fetched £96 and £49, which was a pleasant surprise. Poor Lulu was heartbroken and mooed constantly. The same afternoon Joyce and Alec called in for tea. They were on holiday nearby again.

Next day we went to Barnstaple and were surprised by the arrival of Margaret Thatcher in the pannier market. She was so much more attractive than she had appeared to be on television or in the press – a lovely complexion and quite radiant and happy. Myra came for a four-day visit the same afternoon and was sorry to have missed Mrs Thatcher.

The next excitement was walking the sheep and lambs for dipping. I had to walk ahead, with the sheep following, and with John and Bess behind. I was so scared they would go past me and race down to the busy main road. Fortunately David knew we were coming and he was out in the road to join me and help us across the main road and up the lane opposite to Roy Ley's dip. We were lucky not to meet a car in our road, and it was the same on our return. I wouldn't like that ordeal too often.

Now, Arthur Adams had asked John to milk for him for a week while he was on holiday. One day when John was recording then going straight on to Arthur's, I noticed six bullocks in the garden. It took me nearly an hour to get them back to their field. Bess was useless; I finally shut her in and did better on my own.

The family arrived one weekend, bringing their rabbits, Flopsy and Mopsy, who enjoyed their holiday in the lamb shed. We were all inspecting the sheep one day when Sylvester, very friendly with Michael, suddenly turned aggressive and thumped him hard. 'That settles it,' I said, 'he's had his last chance, now he's going to market.' He went that same week and soon managed to jump in with a pen of ewes! He fetched £90 – not bad for a £7 tame lamb. He was an excellent young ram, but I was glad to see the back of him.

There were gales in late December, blowing galvanized sections off the lamb shed and top shed, but John was able to fix these back on.

Not too bad a year, on the whole…

Chapter X

1980

We started the New Year with the resolution to redecorate our bedroom. We moved our bed into the middle room and John started peeling off wallpaper and ceiling tiles. We decided January was the best time for decorating, as the lambing was not due to start until February and the weather was usually too bad for working outside. It was certainly cold but surprisingly dry, which meant that with recording, relief milking and some outside work we had to leave the bedroom for a while.

We picked up two weaners from a farmer in Middle Marwood and at the same time sent our two previous ones to the abattoir. We did quite well buying these young pigs and fattening them, as nearly all made quality grade so fetched good prices.

We had a nasty shock on 22nd January when John discovered a ewe with afterbirth but no lamb. It was at least two weeks before she was due. He fetched Joy, as she was an expert at lambing, but she couldn't help us, as it was a case of ringwomb. We sent for the vet who was able to remove the lamb. It was only just alive, but his mother ignored him and he died soon after. A bad start!

All the ewes were lambing early; we had a second ringwomb, which we took into the vet in the trailer, and two further abortions. We lost six lambs altogether as two of these were doubles. When we spoke to other farmers later we discovered that Denzil had had similar trouble and another had his first twelve ewes abort. Fortunately, the rest of ours were all right and we finally had twenty-seven lambs living – ten doubles and seven singles, which wasn't too bad. We decided we couldn't face this lambing trauma again and sold the lot as couples in March, getting £60 for double couples and £50 for singles. Sam was pleased to announce that Sylvester had 'served' about twelve of his ewes when he had broken through to them earlier on, and they were producing double couples.

In March we bought a small, pretty piano in Barnstaple for £60. We were able to bring it home in the car trailer. Cleaned and polished it looked really beautiful. It was a French piano by A Bord, Victorian, and dating from about 1880. It needed tuning, of course. The family enjoyed it when they came and it was useful in the wet weather. Michael had started lessons, rather reluctantly, and whenever he was persuaded to practise Catherine would start thumping on the top keys, so was reprimanded. This was amusing, in retrospect, as Michael soon gave up playing while Catherine eventually became a very talented pianist

Now we were able to continue with our decorating whenever we found some spare time. It was the end of April when the carpet was finally fitted and the curtains, which I had made, were hung. It was good to move back in. The kitchen was next on our agenda, but that would have to wait.

We were still buying weaner pigs and calves. There was usually at least one calf in a batch which refused to drink from a bucket. This time there were two that had to go to Lulu. I had good regular orders for cream, butter and cheese, so I was annoyed at getting no milk.

Florence, who had been willing to feed calves, had decided to get mastitis in one quarter and ran a high temperature, so she was useless. It was a relief when I could finally inform my customers that I was in dairy production again.

This was a busy time in the garden again and, apart from planting and sowing seed, John put three plum and six apple trees in the orchard.

Shandy brought in three baby rabbits within a few days. We didn't notice the big rabbits around and had no time to go looking for them. Luckily for us, Fred was happy to come shooting here, or at Collins, so he often brought us in a couple and sometimes a pheasant.

In May we sorted out our best seven bullocks for the South Molton stores sale. We went to watch them being sold and were delighted to get £1,831 for them. We visited Uncle Ken at the weekend to tell him of this and other good news. He was really proud of John, as he had not expected him to do so well with farming. Although he had not helped us with money or advice, the fact that he had done the same as us when he and Dolly were middle-aged had certainly influenced and encouraged us into our present lifestyle.

Our family arrived on 23rd May, complete with a trailer tent, which they erected at the top of Lane Field. Michael was pleased to tell us he had obtained three golds in the Gordano District Cubs' swimming gala, also a silver for Cubs' six-aside football. Iain was soon busy servicing the tractor and servicing the mower and spinner, while Maggie was busy on the piano!

There was plenty of rain on the spring Bank Holiday and John, Maggie (in an overall and her dad's cap) and Iain knocked down the kitchen ceiling. It had been a terrible eyesore; all bumps and hollows. This job created dreadful dirt and mess and almost choked them! (I was entertaining the children elsewhere.) They all went home the next day.

The next job was stripping the wallpaper. This was most intriguing, as we discovered very old newspapers lining the walls underneath, but a terrible time waster, as we just couldn't resist reading them! John now fixed insulating board on the ceiling and walls, then he sealed the ceiling while I did the walls, and these were then lined, papered and painted. The woodwork was a longer job, and included the kitchen cabinets, but at last the yellow topcoat was on and the improvement was amazing. The ceiling no longer looked so low, as it was level and light. With pretty new curtains and Marley Vinylaire on the floor, I now felt happier about spending so much time in the kitchen.

We started haymaking at the end of June. David cut the grass in Hill field and Bill Pincombe baled – 593 bales. Three fields at Collins then yielded 898 bales. It was an anxious time this year because of occasional heavy rain, but it was a good result in the end.

We collected Michael and Catherine from Nailsea on 2nd August. We had rain every day for a week, which was not much fun for the children but was a busy week for us. Tim was collected for the abattoir and we had a hindquarter back for the freezer a few days later. The beef was absolutely delicious and very tender.

Our latest cow, Annabel, calved on the Wednesday – a Charolais X Jersey heifer. On the same day Sam and family went off for a ten-day holiday, leaving us in charge of their farm. We also had Rosalyn's dog, Sophie, with her six puppies, to look after. John had to put Sam's calves on his cows after hand-milking enough for Mrs Wright. There was one rather miserable calf that Sam had said was no good and possibly a 'die-er'. We made a big fuss of him and gave him priority with the milk. He responded immediately, became really lively, and Sam was most surprised when he saw him again after just ten days.

In answer to our advertisement in the local paper we were offered a 30 ft by 10 ft fowl house. As it was a fine warm day for a change we took the children to High Bickington to have a look at it. We were very impressed, apart from the difficulty of dismantling, so we decided to think about it.

Now Lulu calved, eleven days early; a good Devon X bull calf, very strong on his legs. He would be company for Annabel's calf, who was doing well. We received the cheque for Tim – almost £400, which, considering we had a hindquarter back for ourselves, was very good.

We heard of another fowl house for sale at a farm near Lapford, so off we went to look at that. It was only an 8 ft by 6 ft, but in very good condition and was just £20. We bought it and would collect it later. We were still considering the big one. When the family arrived John and Iain went to see if this could be dismantled and collected. They decided it could and paid £125. Next day off they all went – I was allowed to stay home to get the dinner, and I was lucky as poor Maggie was covered in fleabites. A couple of days later John and Iain finished bringing it home. It took them all day. It was about four weeks before the erection was started.

At the end of August we made a little hay at the top of Lane Field. Fred bought and collected the 172 bales. During this haymaking we bought thirty store lambs at

Blackmoor Gate. We bought a further thirty-four two weeks later. We trimmed and sprayed their feet and drenched and vaccinated them.

John was doing holiday relief for Brian again. I made my first cheese since June, and was still busy with butter and cream. I also made tomato ketchup – which was delicious – as we had a huge crop of tomatoes in the greenhouse. I had also put creosote on the small fowl house and cleaned all our windows inside and out. I was able to do the upstairs ones easily from inside, which was lucky as I was terrified of ladders!

In mid-September Joyce and Alec visited again, bringing their friends, Ken and Brenda, with them. We enjoyed their visit and I think they were fascinated to watch us removing maggots from two of the lambs!

We took our two calves to South Molton market. Annabel's Charolais heifer fetched £76 and Lulu's Devon bull £119. Lulu really was amazing, especially as she and Tim were Betsy's calves. People turned up their noses at Betsy when we bought her – a frisky, small Jersey with horns – but she produced some very worthwhile offspring.

John levelled a site in the orchard in readiness for the big fowl house and he and Iain spent the next two days erecting it. It was wet most of the time and Iain had to return home before the roofing sheets were fixed. John finally completed this, fixed the windows and we creosoted it inside and out. We called it the 'village hall'! Twenty-four maran pullets were soon installed and laid us plenty of eggs.

In October we bought ten young pigs at Exeter market for £222. We had our trailer fixed at the exit, the tailboard down ready, so the loading should have been simple.

However, three of the pigs decided to run under the trailer and chase around in the car park between moving vehicles, gradually making their way toward the main road. It was a frightening experience, keeping the other seven in the trailer while we tried to capture the three escapees. Eventually, with the assistance of market staff, we managed to load them safely. When we sent them to the abattoir seven weeks later they were all quality graded, but rather a disappointing price as market prices had dropped over all. We decided to have a rest from pigs for the time being.

In November our old freezer packed up. It was about fourteen years old and we had brought it with us from our bungalow. We needed two freezers so we went straight to Mole Valley Farmers for a replacement one, which we collected.

On 19th December our family arrived for a short visit. On the Sunday we had our Christmas dinner with them. Maggie, Michael and I fed three new calves in the pigsty and had fun and games with them. They went home the next day. On Christmas Eve we went to Uncle Ken's for dinner and exchanged gifts. It was a lovely visit, as usual.

Chapter XI
1981

We were fortunate to have no snow in January. On the 3rd there was a fox shoot, organised by Sam. They shot five foxes in the woods below us. Later John and I spent the evening with Denzil and Beryl and had a very enjoyable time, somewhat marred by getting a puncture on the way home. John was changing the wheel around midnight in a dark country lane with a howling wind blowing.

A few days later John and Denzil went on a sheep assessment course, firstly at Roundswell and then to see a film at the Imperial Hotel in Barnstaple. They finished up with fish and chips at The Pelican, Sticklepath. All right for some! Next they went on a mole course together, and John had a certificate entitling him to purchase strychnine for killing moles. Actually we had little trouble with them at Kinnings, but John was able to help Michael Cork, whose farm he visited for milk recording.

In February and March we were busy buying calves and tame lambs and Florence produced a good heifer calf. John helped David on several occasions, clearing his wood, and was able to bring home wood for our fires.

There was very heavy rain in March and on the 10th there was flooding. Several roads were closed and Edwin Fewings lost eighteen hoggs in his fields adjacent to the river.

We had already purchased thirty tame lambs when Fred gave me a good Suffolk ram lamb. Some of these lambs were very young and sometimes weakly. We found that cows colostrum suited them well and always kept some in the freezer. David provided some when his cows calved.

Our family arrived on 10th April, with Maggie proud to tell us she was now a qualified lifesaver. Iain was soon busy repairing machinery and helping to dismantle the old hay barn, which had now completely collapsed. This resulted in a good bonfire, which the children loved. Catherine was now entertaining us on the piano. It was amazing how well she was playing after only a few lessons. Michael was a Scout now and did lots of extra jobs for Scout Week.

We sent ten bullocks to South Molton market in May and were well pleased when they fetched £286 each. We were also pleased that our hens were laying very well – forty-three eggs in a day, which was a record. All our store hoggs were now sold. They didn't make a very good profit so we decided not to bother with them again. We preferred the baby lambs as it was so rewarding to care for these little orphans.

During May we had trouble with bullocks coming into Collins fields from Chapples. This happened on several occasions, and I was tired of phoning to complain. At least we weren't so troubled now with animals breaking into Kinnings. These hedges had been so neglected in the past that it was difficult to make them stock-proof.

We were busy gardening and I was upset to find all my peas had been pecked out, probably by mice. John was busy in the fields, dung spreading, chain-harrowing, fertilising and rolling. We were hoping to get a baler this year, and finally found one near Torrington that would suit us.

Once again there was trouble in the house! The immersion heater had corroded and water was leaking from the top of the cylinder and coming through the kitchen ceiling. We discovered that our plumber had been off work for six weeks and was unable to drive. However, with John fetching him, he was kind enough to fit a new heater for us.

We started haymaking on 19th June and John cut the grass with a Fahr 20 mower and was able to do his own baling. Although the weather was unsettled, as usual, we managed to get through it all in fairly good time. We were able to spare 114 bales for Fred, who had now put some sheep at Collins. He sheared our lambs later.

On 30th June we sent our first three lambs to the abattoir and they fetched £97. We now had thirty-four altogether, and all lived this time. Taking expenses into account we made about £20 profit per lamb, which was excellent. I must admit we had three of them given to us, two of these not expected to live, but they did.

July started off quite well. The council had cut back the hedges in the road and it was now resurfaced. I picked lots of strawberries from the garden. We bought a David Brown 990 tractor. It was good that we could afford some better machinery at last. I did have a nasty shock one afternoon when I saw a large grass snake – at least 3 ft long – curled up in the sun, by the front door. I shrieked and went back in the house! We had no idea they grew to this size. Later we saw plenty of small ones, which Michael and Catherine would play with. Ugh!

We had some terrible news on the 23rd. Beryl rang to

say Denzil had leukaemia. She was crying and very distressed. He was in Barnstaple hospital, having driven in there himself on the advice of his doctor, and was very ill. We had been chatting to him in the market a few days before, so it was a dreadful shock, especially to Beryl. We took her to visit him next day, as she didn't drive. He had a single room with TV and washbasin and special drugs had been sent for.

Two days later Brian rang to say his father was much worse. Beryl rang another day to say he had improved, but when we visited him next he could hardly speak and looked terrible. Beryl was sleeping in the hospital. The next day she rang to say there was improvement again, but two days later he had passed away. He had been a special friend to us, and we were incredibly sad and very shocked at the suddenness of it all. We attended his funeral at Chittlehampton. The church was packed with neighbours and friends. We kept in close touch with Beryl and usually took her to Barnstaple on Fridays. In the meantime she had driving lessons and finally passed her test. She was very brave.

Lulu calved at the end of July – a strong bull calf. It was her fifth bull in four calvings and fetched £120. Annabel calved later, a heifer calf – £73. More lambs and pigs were going to the abattoir and we were buying more weaners. All were doing well.

In September we took the remaining lambs in David's trailer to be dipped. They thoroughly enjoyed the outing, especially the dipping part. They were jumping in for second gos! Roy was not amused as he was in a hurry, with two more lots to do after ours. These young animals always surprised us with their antics.

Recently we had come across two of our young

bullocks having a fight, while the rest were very interested and stood around watching them. Another time, when we were showing some visitors our pigs, the animals decided to put on a boxing display. All four of them stood on their hind legs and gently attacked each other. It was an unbelievable sight, and very funny!

Several of the older hens had now stopped laying and were killed off for the table. We bought forty Warren pullets from Mortonhampstead and put them in the 'village hall'. We still had fourteen older ones outside, and the fox came at dusk one evening and scattered them just before they were shut in for the night. We could only find ten, but three more returned during the next day. Finally John spotted the fourteenth and eventually caught her a day later, and all were now kept in their house permanently. We were lucky not to lose any after the frantic squawking we heard from the meadow.

Fred removed his sheep from Collins on 11th October. They had been there for five weeks. He also took Hurricane, our young ram, to look after him for us during the winter so we were then able to keep our ewes and wethers together again (the wethers are castrated rams). We went to Withypool after tea on 18th October and found Aunty Dolly in bed very poorly. We put clean sheets on both their beds and did what we could for her. It was difficult being so far away, especially when John was so busy and I couldn't drive. We visited again in November, and Aunty was up but she was still very weak.

We were buying calves during November, mainly through John May, but they were very expensive at this time. However, when we were bringing our bullocks back from Collins we passed Frank Congram, who showed an interest in them. On closer inspection he decided to buy and gave a fair price for them.

There was plenty of rain in early December. In fact, it had been a fairly wet year altogether, and the first year John had not needed to fetch water from the river.

We had a little snow on the 9th and 10th. We had hoped to go to Maggie's on Sunday, but the forecast was so bad by Saturday evening that we had to phone and cancel. Just as well, as it was a terrible day: a blizzard and heavy snowfall. Later there was torrential rain, gales and flooding. The electricity was off at eleven o'clock and wasn't restored until one o'clock the following day. We had to get our eight remaining lambs into the old shippen. John didn't milk the cows on Sunday afternoon, but on Monday morning he put calves on two of the cows and hand-milked Lulu. On Tuesday the power was off again from nine in the morning until gone nine at night.

We went to Nailsea on the 19th but had to leave for home at two o'clock because snow was forecast again. Luckily we had only rain and gales. Anyway, we had the chance to exchange presents at least.

On the 23rd Sam put forty-five ewes at Collins. Next day we went to Withypool for a short visit. Aunty was still very poorly and getting confused. She asked if we had a cow!

On Christmas day we rang Beryl and Maggie. We lit a log fire in the dining room and enjoyed a turkey dinner there, just the two of us. We walked to Collins in the afternoon, then called on Sam and Rosalyn and stayed for a while sampling their apple wine and Samantha's Christmas cake. The year ended quietly.

Chapter XII
1982

January began with cold and mainly wet weather. We managed to get to Hatherleigh on the 5th and bought our first tame lamb. Two days later, when Ian Waldron came to collect three tons of hay from us, he brought us a tiny black lamb, so we were starting earlier with them this year.

The same evening it snowed and everything was white when we went to bed. Next morning our road was blocked with frozen snow, so John was unable to finish his milk recording at Atherington. We lost the power at eight forty-five, as expected. It only needed a fall of snow or a clap of thunder at Kinnings and off it went. All the roads in Devon were frozen and there was further heavy snow. Also the phone was out of order!

After four days of absolute misery the power and phone were back on. Anxiously we opened the freezers and were relieved to find the meat still frozen. The ice cream had to be thrown out, but other smaller items such as sausages, which had almost thawed, had to be cooked and then refrozen. We were amazed to discover the council using a bulldozer on our road for the two days following. Five lambs came across to us from Sam, all very cold and one very weak. Although we did our best for them, only one survived.

Later in the month when it became milder we bought ten lambs from Hatherleigh, averaging £8 each. One of these was bigger, stronger and wilder than the rest and kept jumping out of the lamb pen to get in with the ewes. He was so persistent that a woman, watching him, remarked, 'Bless him, he wants a drop of titty!' I was worried that he might upset the smaller lambs on the way home so had him in the front of the car with me. He immediately lay across my lap and slept throughout the journey! He was never any trouble and I really fell in love with him. I called him Jeremiah as the rams were on biblical names that year. When John was recording I had to bottle feed the sixteen, which took me an hour and a quarter.

On 15th February Uncle Ken rang to say that Dolly had passed away, which was very upsetting news. She had been very weak for some months, but even though he expected it he missed her so much. John went across and spent a couple of hours with him. I was suffering from very painful sciatica for some days, so John had to attend her cremation alone.

We were still buying lambs and had forty-eight altogether that year. It was like a hospital with penicillin, scour mixture, terramycin, maggot fly spray, drenches, cod liver oil and glucose. We also had to provide bottles and teats, milk, straw, sheep nuts and pellets, marking spray and dipping and veterinary treatment, all of which averaged £5 per lamb.

Florence calved – an Angus bull calf that made £60. I had not been selling butter or cream for a while as we had insufficient milk, but now I was able to start again.

The family arrived at teatime on Good Friday. Michael had passed his canoeing test for Scouts that morning. Catherine, who had played the piano in the Bristol Eisteddfod, was proud to show us her certificate for third place. We had two of our lambs buried that day, so the children's news helped cheer us up. They all went home on the Tuesday, but on Thursday Maggie phoned with upsetting news. Iain's father had died in hospital after a heart attack the day before. This was unexpected so a great shock. It was proving to be an unhappy year so far. Louis' funeral was six days later. Maggie rang that evening to tell us about it, but also had good news that Catherine had received first class marks for piano – eighty-five per cent – at the Weston festival.

Meanwhile we had discovered Bluebell lamb with her tail bitten off, possibly by a rat. She was very poorly and refused to drink. John sprayed it and gave her a penicillin injection. It was touch and go for five days, but continuing this treatment and using a syringe to get a little milk into her, she suddenly became bright and eager again and had no further trouble. In fact she made £36.50 finally in Barnstaple market, and as she was given to me by Beryl it was worth our efforts! Of course we couldn't save all of them, but had certainly cured several over the years. We had discovered that sheep could appear quite well one minute then lie down and die the next, which gave no opportunity for treating them.

The family soon turned up again, mainly for Michael's twelfth birthday on 2nd May. He had been given a two-man tent and wanted to try it out on our lawn. Unfortunately, after a sunny day there were showers and strong winds in the evening – the first rain since 7th April! The children went out to sleep in the tent but gave up at eleven o'clock and came back inside to their beds.

We were having trouble with our maran hens as we kept finding their eggs eaten. I couldn't believe that hens were eating their own eggs until I actually saw a maran, sitting in the nest, enjoying one! We started to get rid of them.

We had a splendid crop of potatoes this year, so I was horrified to see Sam's cows and bullocks tramping over them in our orchard. I picked up my stick and rushed out to shoo them back across Well Field. John was milking for David at the time and Bess was missing.

Actually, three weeks later she was missing for real. She disappeared while John was taking three lambs to the abattoir and we thought she must have decided to follow the trailer. I rang South Molton and Barnstaple police stations and the Canine Defence at Braunton as well as many of our neighbours. We drove around High Bickington and Burrington, all to no avail. John couldn't have been busier – relief milking, milk recording, haymaking etc. Then Lulu calved, had milk fever and needed the vet. In the middle of that a man from Burrington rang to say he had Bess there! The reunion was almost indescribable, hugs and tail waggings, but crying as well because she was starving, dirty, and her poor feet so sore after four days of running around the roads. She had obviously followed John, missed him at the main road and taken the turning towards the sheep dip, as she was familiar with that. But she couldn't find her boss and was completely lost. Poor Bess!

The children were staying with us in August. One day they were upstairs with me when we heard a loud buzzing in the bathroom. There was a huge thing flying around there, which I needed to get out of the window – I discovered later it was a hornet. Michael and Catherine shrieked and went running downstairs, leaving me with it. I had hoped for support considering those little devils could handle all kinds of creepy crawlies and the horrible snakes. It took me ages to open the window wider with that thing buzzing angrily around me!

Next day we fetched the bullocks back from Collins for drenching, eye treatment, and fly spray, then returned them. They behaved very well. The twenty-one lambs that went for dipping also behaved themselves this year. We took Lulu's heifer calf to South Molton, putting an £85 reserve on her, but she made £100 so we were well pleased. Lulu was upset at first, but a few days later she gave seven gallons of milk in one day, so had soon recovered.

The haymaking had gone quite well this year, and we had a surplus again to sell. We had also done well with our fruit, vegetables and eggs. Fred brought us pheasants, rabbits and a duck, and we had two pheasants from David. No fear of starving!

When we were fetching our last four store bullocks from Collins ready to send them to market, Bess became very excitable. The bullocks panicked and split up at Gypsy Lane. Two pushed past me and finished up in the nearby garden. Finally all four rushed towards Kinnings but went past the entrance. Then we all panicked! John was climbing hedges and running through fields in an effort to get ahead of them, then a car came up the road at the right time and turned them, so panic over.

In November Terry Sedwell did a considerable amount of hedging for us against Meadow and Lane Fields in order to make it more stock proof. John helped David to plant trees – 200 in just one morning, and a further number on other days.

We made visits to Uncle Ken whenever possible. He was very poorly at times and his face was looking thin, but he was always cheerful when we were there. In December we went to Weymouth to see Aunty Edie, who was now home from hospital. She was very bright and looking quite well. On the journey down we stopped for our flask of coffee overlooking Chesil Beach. It looked beautiful with the sun shining on the water.

We ordered a porch from Leeds to fix outside our front door. It arrived earlier than we expected without warning, and the two men had dinner with us – stuffed marrow and peaches and cream – before erecting it. They had expected to find a café!

The 'village hall' had been empty for some time as we had fewer hens now. It had been thoroughly cleaned and disinfected ready for lambs. The first two had already arrived from Sam – Alice and George. Little George was very wet and cold when he arrived, so after a gentle rub down I put him in a cardboard box and popped him in the oven of the Rayburn for a while. It was late evening and the fire only low so the temperature was just right for him. He soon revived and took a drop of milk. He stayed in the kitchen all night and next day was able to join Alice, who was delighted to have company. These two would count as our 1983 lambs.

This had been a successful year for us. We had bought forty-eight lambs and although we lost nine of them we still made an average profit of £20 per lamb. We were very pleased with the prices we received for young calves, averaging £127, and for the store cattle, averaging £300. We sold hay and keep, eggs and dairy produce. We transported animals to and from market with our trailer and John did his milk recording and other outside jobs. It was hard work, with no holidays, but we loved it.

Chapter XIII
1983

On 1st January a farmer in Chawleigh rang offering us two tame lambs. Fortunately we were ready to take them as we had already installed Alice and George in the 'village hall'. We collected them late in the evening and they all settled down happily together. The next day John fixed an electric light there, which made it easier for the evening feeds. We finished up with twenty-four lambs by the end of January; an unusually early start.

We had a shock on the 4th when, after gales had given us a sleepless night, we awoke to discover no water in the taps. John was due to milk for David in the morning so we had to wait until later in the day for him to change the pump. Next day Jane calved – a Hereford x heifer calf – with no complications.

It was exciting on the 6th to have our generator fixed at last. We were delighted to find it worked all our appliances in the house as well as the milking machine, so we would no longer be troubled with power cuts. If only we could have afforded it earlier on!

One of the difficulties with rearing tame lambs was getting some of them to drink from the bottle. I used to nurse them and encourage them gently and they usually responded. Edwin was a strong, stubborn lamb, so John took him on. He fiddled about with the bottle for four days, giving an occasional suck, but the milk was mostly poured down with him sitting on his bottom!

However, on the fifth day he decided to stand up and enjoy his bottle, sucking hard and very loudly. He was the first to go fat to market, with Alice. By 22nd February we were bottle-feeding thirty-seven lambs three times a day using 5½ gallons of milk.

On the 23rd John milked for David for the last time as he was giving up dairying at the end of the month. He still continued to help him with other jobs.

Florence calved on 10th March – a Charolais heifer which made £85. Unfortunately she had milk fever later, and the vet arrived before breakfast to inject her. Also Jane needed an injection too, as she was not getting in calf.

We were already having to refuse lambs now as we had forty-nine living, five having died. One person was very disappointed and mentioned that the NFU were inundated with them this year. Four of our last ones were given to us – one from Beryl and three from Fred after he finished his keep at Collins – so we couldn't refuse those! They were more expensive to buy this year, averaging £8 each.

Our family came on 1st April for the Easter weekend and helped with feeding the lambs. Maggie took over the newest tiny one who was needing four bottles a day. Michael helped John dose the calves with Dictol and also to clear the back shippen. He also cleaned my brass in the house. He earned four pounds in job week money for the Scouts. Iain dug a trench and collected stones in readiness for building a wall – a busy time all round, and reasonable weather for a change.

In May Michael and Catherine slept out in the tent one night, despite a wet day. We now had to start buying in calves as we had surplus milk with Florence milking well and many lambs now weaned. At South Molton even mediocre heifers were fetching silly prices, but we were luckier at Barnstaple next day, getting two heifers for £35 and £51. Then Beryl sold us a heifer and a bull for £65 the pair.

Throughout May we were busy gardening. I spring-cleaned through the house. John fitted a window in the bottom end of the old shippen, which made it much lighter. David gave us a banty sitting on guinea fowl eggs. Recording for Edwin one evening, John didn't arrive home until nearly ten o'clock. He had been helping to raise a sick cow with an inflatable mattress, hired for £5 a day. These cost approximately £200, with motor. Another evening we had a power cut so used our generator again.

There was a general election on 9th June. I stayed up until one fifteen for the early results. Finally, the Conservatives were in with a huge majority, about 145 seats overall.

John started cutting grass at Collins. It had grown well because of plenty of rain during May. There was a terrible amount of weed at Collins. Every time John rowed up I went around picking out as many thistles, docks and nettles as I could see, a back-aching job, and I must have walked miles! We had already got rid of loads of bracken by pulling it out by hand where it had newly emerged – we even had the children helping with this. Cutting down and burning it didn't get rid of it, and it then had to be removed anyway because of it's danger to animals, being poisonous.

A racing pigeon arrived one day, quite exhausted and probably blown off course. It was grateful for water and corn and stayed quite a time. On the twelfth day, when it seemed really strong and well, we shooed it gently away and told it to go home. It must have found the way, as it didn't return.

July started off very hot and sunny. Maggie rang on the 6th to say Nan (John's mother) had had a heart attack and was unconscious. We heard later she had recovered, but on the 12th Maggie rang us late to say Nan had died that evening, which was very upsetting news. The funeral was a week later in the morning. John went off early to Bristol, calling on Maggie on the way. I stayed on the farm to feed the calves and to see to other necessary jobs.

With Aunty Edie frequently in and out of hospital in Weymouth, Ted, my brother, likewise in Bristol and the death of our friend Clarice, this had not been a happy year so far.

Lulu calved in July – a beautiful Charolais bull calf which fetched £201 in South Molton market. The lambs were dipped by Roy Ley, having earlier been sheared by Sam. John was fetching water from the river again as the weather remained very dry and warm. The cows and bullocks were being fed the new hay, as grass was not growing.

Mr Wright had struck water in their meadow – an overflow from their well – and diverted it to our orchard nearby. It trickled through and we were able to collect some for a while but it eventually dried up in August.

Annabel calved in August, a Charolais bull calf, which we decided to rear. We took the children to Withypool one day and enjoyed a picnic lunch on the riverbank. Afterwards they enjoyed playing in the water with Bess. Uncle Ken was looking quite well this time and enjoying the company of his campers.

We took five lambs to South Molton and found the prices disastrous, only getting £79.68. Fortunately, a guaranteed price was in force, giving us an extra premium. This amounted to £87.67, so added to the selling price, it was very good. This continued throughout this year and the next, so we did very well with lambs.

We were having rain again by 20th August after a very hot spell, so our well soon filled again and some mushrooms appeared. Michael helped John collect 235 bales of golden straw from Beers.

We were buying calves during September and October, many from the markets and later from Beryl. They kept us busy, feeding them, cleaning them out and moving them about. We decided to sell some as weaned calves between three and four months old, which meant we could keep them housed. We were selling bullocks at Barnstaple and South Molton and were well pleased with the prices. At the end of October we picked our last cucumber. We had over fifty from one 45 p plant! The tomatoes and cucumbers always did well in our greenhouse.

We bought a few more calves in November. John and I usually fed them together, but I had the job alone when John was milk recording. I fed twenty-three calves one day. They were impatient and kept bellowing!

One morning a lamb was loose in our lane and brought the cows down for milking. 'Quicker than I can,' said John! It was a comical sight to see three cows walking sedately behind a little lamb all the way to the shippen.

December was uneventful until Christmas. We had a guinea fowl for our Christmas dinner, which made a tasty change. We were expecting Jane to calve, but she left it until Boxing Day, when she produced a good Hereford X bull calf, which fetched £146 in January.

On the 28th John killed two guinea fowls and I plucked them. One of the others escaped from the house, playing safe? We didn't expect to catch him, but two days later John, Iain and the children managed to trap him at dusk and returned him to the house with the others. On the 30th John gave Bess a bath so she was all clean and ready for the New Year.

Chapter XIV
1984

January was a month of gales, heavy storms and hail, with just the occasional dry, sunny day in between. The family were staying for the New Year and helped us fetch the lambs home from Collins. They raced along the road like greyhounds!

Next day the vet came for TB and blood tests for the cattle (forty including calves). They were all very good except Florence, who made a great fuss. The results were okay. Shandy had not been well lately, so the vet examined him on the kitchen table with all of us watching anxiously, and we were told his kidneys were enlarged. The prescribed tablets did no good and he became so poorly that we had him put to sleep at the end of the month. I was very sad and tearful, as he was a very special pet and we missed him so much. We still had Suzie, but she disappeared most of the time, just turning up for meals.

When we were cleaning through the 'village hall' we spotted a large rat at the other end. I was out of there in a second, but Bess went in and killed it for us. We then finished cleaning and disinfecting.

In February we visited Fred and Joy in the house they had recently bought in Burrington. We were very impressed, especially with the land attached and the stream running through the back.

We bought our first tame lambs on 10th February,

much later than last year. They were fetching very high prices so we had to be careful. When we arrived home we found Florence had calved – a black Angus bull calf. Both were well. At the end of February we bought twelve Tetra pullets from Whiddon farmhouse – a new kind of bird for us.

We eventually bought several lambs during February and early March, mostly from markets, but five from Michael Cork and two from Sam. On 13th March we were up at five forty-five to feed them before John went milk recording. We were very shocked to find little George dead. He had been a strong, lively lamb, with us for two weeks and needing no treatments. Just four days later we found another lamb lying out dead first thing. We had not had any trouble with her either, so it was a mystery. The lambs were getting orf again and the orfoids didn't really help, but a vaccine recommended by another farmer was very satisfactory and soon cleared it up.

March had been a cold month but mainly dry, so we were relieved to get some rain towards the end. The pheasants and pigeons were busy eating our spring cabbage plants, so John put wire over to protect them. They had already had the purple sprouting!

April started off quite dry. We were hoping to get our cows to Collins, but there was hardly a blade of grass there. We badly needed some rain. However, it meant we could work outside. John was clearing the top garden ready for some of the lambs as well as spreading dung, then fertiliser on Hill Field. We had a little rain the following morning which helped, but the rest of the month was fine and sunny. John planted two trays of potatoes while I pricked out cabbage and lettuce seedlings.

We had not heard from Aunty Edie for some time so I rang Geoff Bailey, her friendly neighbour, for news of her. She had been in Westhaven hospital, Weymouth, since the end of December and nobody had told us. I immediately wrote to her, promising we would visit as soon as possible.

On 12th May Michael set off for his first Ten Tors expedition on Dartmoor. About 2,500 people set off from Okehampton. We were busy in the garden that day. John dug his bean trench while I washed inside the greenhouse with Jeyes Fluid. We visited Uncle Ken in the evening. The next day Michael rang in the afternoon to say he had arrived back at Okehampton before ten o'clock and received his bronze medal for thirty-five miles. Maggie and Iain went to welcome him in.

We next heard that Edie had been told she would not be returning to her flat. Her furniture and other effects had to be removed and sold. When we visited her she insisted that we dealt with this. Goodness knows how we could manage to make several visits to Weymouth as well as our farm work, but we did! We met her solicitor and the Dorchester auctioneer, sorted and distributed many items and brought other things back in the trailer, visiting a very unhappy Edie as well. We made our final visit on 10th June, just in time for John to cut the grass the next day in readiness for haymaking.

During this time plenty had been happening at Kinnings. We had received another sitting of guinea fowl eggs from David. One morning John announced, 'There's a peacock walking up the lane!' I thought he was joking until I saw it myself. It stayed with us for a couple of days, flying into the lambs' enclosure and eating their food or sitting on the bonnet of our car, its favourite place. We couldn't trace its owner, but it eventually disappeared, we think towards the nearby village of Warkleigh.

On 28th May David rang to say his mother had had a stroke and was in hospital. She returned home two days later, physically well but very confused.

After dark one evening we heard a rumpus in the meadow and discovered that three horses and sixteen of Peter Hedges' bullocks had jumped over the hedge and joined our twenty-three. Peter came over and helped John to get all the bullocks into our cubicle house until they could be sorted out in daylight. I can't remember what happened to the horses. They were owned by a Mrs Harris who had recently bought the land.

The haymaking went off fairly well as the weather was good, but we had to rely on David for the baling as the knotting had gone wrong on our baler. We made almost 1,000 bales altogether. We had to stop then as the weathermen told us there would be no rain for thirty days and we needed the grass.

Lulu calved on 8th July, a good Charolais bull calf. She was our seventh calver. When her calf fetched £171, it was the highest calf price that day in South Molton market.

We bought a black Jersey X in-calf heifer at Hatherleigh for £197. She had horns, which made Florence and the other cows nervous of her, so she was able to settle in without being pushed around. We called her Betsy II. We sent Annabel off barren to Barnstaple market where she fetched £166 – not too bad for a Jersey.

John left the gate of Lane Field open one night. Next morning we discovered the cows in the garden where they had eaten and trampled the cabbages. I don't know why we bothered to grow them! Never mind, our new apple trees were laden with fruit, the branches almost touching the ground.

The family arrived on Sunday, but Maggie and Iain left on Tuesday, leaving the children for their August holiday with us. It started with the four of us cleaning out three cubicles. Many hands certainly make light (or in this case lighter) work. It wasn't all work for them, though, as we played table tennis on the extending dining table, which was good fun.

On a warm sunny afternoon we walked through David's fields alongside the river towards the Portsmouth Arms. The children paddled in the water and Bess enjoyed it too. Another day we all went up to the caravan site to burn the remains of the caravan – bonfires being a great favourite. A man had previously bought the caravan but had only removed the aluminium from it, so it was good to get the remainder cleared away.

One afternoon we heard Florence bawling at something over the hedge from Lane Field. We discovered there was a heifer in calving difficulties and immediately rang the owner. The calf was stuck half way out, still in the bag and dead. If Florence hadn't raised the alarm it is possible the heifer would eventually have died as well.

Our separator had been out of order for a while, and as we now had milk spare for cream and butter we decided to buy a new one, which had been recommended to us. We soon had orders again.

The family were here again at the end of August helping to pick blackberries – at least 12 lbs – and to pick and prepare loads of runner beans for the freezer. John dug potatoes from the garden and orchard, surprised at the good crop after such dry weather. We had plenty to last us for the winter. A little drizzle had encouraged mushrooms to appear at Collins.

We were still buying and selling calves, also selling lambs. We also bought a Friesian heifer at a farm sale and called her Edie. This was on Aunty's instructions, as she wanted us to use some of the money from the sale of her furniture to buy a cow.

September was a quiet month. We had plenty of frogs in the garden. Jane had pneumonia and the vet didn't expect her to recover, but she did. The lambs went for dipping while I stayed with Beth, who had recovered fairly well from her stroke.

In October Betsy II calved – a small brown heifer. We went to a tea party at the village hall (the real one!), which was very enjoyable. We had very sad news on the 12th when David rang to say that Beth had passed away last evening. I knew I would miss my good friend very much. John went to her funeral in Barnstaple. Unfortunately he had to stop at Cobbaton on the way home for milk recording, so I couldn't go with him.

We sent seventeen store cattle to the special sale in South Molton. They sold in two batches – seven made £256 each and ten made £231 each. We had recently sold our five best steers privately for £265 each.

We found two of our lambs dead at Collins in November within a few days of each other, so we brought the rest back home where we could keep an eye on them. We took nine to market where they graded at 20k and fetched £37.80 each plus the premium. It was all ups and down in farming. Jane became very poorly again so this time we had her collected as a casualty. We went to Taunton and bought a Friesian heifer (Kerry) for £400 to replace her.

We had a pleasant surprise when Uncle Ken invited himself to dinner one Sunday. He was so pleased to see our animals and the improvements we had made. I was sorry he missed all our larger bullocks.

The family came on 29th December. We were amused to notice how enormous the children looked now in our low-ceilinged house. Michael had to stoop to go into the kitchen!

Chapter XV
1985

We had a cold start to 1985; heavy frost daily, with taps frozen and a burst pipe. There was some snow on a couple of days, resulting in an icy road, and our lane was like a skating rink. Fortunately I was able to walk across the field to make my usual Wednesday visit to Mrs Wright. Florence fell down outside the cubicle house, which was worrying as she was shortly due to calve. Later in the month we had further snow, which made several roads in North Devon impassable for a while and interfered with John's milk recording. Once again it cleared quite quickly.

Florence calved on the 22nd – a Simmental bull calf. There were no ill effects from her recent fall. Our little Jersey, Nutmeg, was not so lucky, as she had a stillborn calf on the 30th.

John was busy outside, spreading loads of dung and sawing wood for the fires. Inside we were in the process of redecorating our dining room. This would probably take weeks to complete. Even stripping off the old wallpaper had revealed that there were five or six layers to be removed.

We had decided against buying tame lambs this year, but we were buying extra calves and selling weaned ones at three to four months. When Bambi was born to Betsy last year we had decided to rear her rather than get a low price for her at market, but she was rather a lonely creature. On 1st February we bought a young Jersey heifer, Heidi, about seven months old, as company for her and they were very happy together.

We had some excitement in early March, when police with dogs were searching our fields for a youth who had absconded from Newton Abbot remand home. A helicopter came down twice in Sam's field and a policeman, with an Alsatian, called on us. Bess was delighted to see another dog and immediately made friends with it. When they started to gambol around together the policeman lost his temper. 'Get that animal shut away,' he shouted at us. 'I've got a job to do here.' He was so unpleasant that I hoped the boy wouldn't be found, but of course he soon was.

The hens were laying well. One day we had twenty-five eggs from twenty-seven birds. We were able to sell eggs to friends and neighbours and all the surplus to the village shop. I still made butter and cream, but had long since finished with cheese making. We loved the cheese, but we had such trouble storing it, as it was vital to have the correct temperatures. Most were perfect, but occasionally they spoiled. I was busy enough with marmalade, jams, chutneys, and, when we had a glut of tomatoes, ketchup.

We had more snowstorms during March, but each time the sun soon melted it. We continued our work on the dining room and finally completed it on 31st March – all re-papered, painted and with new curtains. It looked very fresh and smart.

One morning in April we found a little heifer calf with her head stuck under the next cubicle. Her nose was bleeding and when we released her we saw a big lump under her throat the size of a tennis ball! That evening a big calf was stuck in the water trough and Sam and Christopher came to the rescue. Three days later the heifer's lump burst and loads of muck came out of it. It hadn't caused her any discomfort, but we were relieved to see it gone.

Edie calved during the night with a Charolais bull calf. It wasn't very big, but when we sent it to the market a couple of week later it fetched £190. We also sent Stewart, a Charolais X Jersey. At twenty months he fetched £454.

On a fine, sunny day in early May we put Bambi and Heidi down in Meadow. The previous day we had put the bullocks in the yard outside the cubicle house to get them used to the electric wire. Now they were also ready for Meadow. They were very reluctant to go at first, but once there they started chasing the girls and upsetting them. Then they discovered the grass so played no more!

Next time we visited Uncle Ken he asked us to clear out his food cupboard. It's a good thing we did, as many items had gone off and others were past their use-by dates. He asked me to visit again soon and spend a whole day with him, sorting other things out and going through Aunty Dolly's treasures. John was just starting his haymaking so I had to wait a while before I could have a day off. I chose a fine, sunny day and Uncle and I had a really enjoyable time together, sorting through things and discarding anything he didn't want. He opened the window of his smallest room upstairs and threw out all the rubbish onto the lawn below. We were laughing and he said he felt better than he had done for a long time. It was fairly late when John arrived to collect me. He was tired after a very busy day and wouldn't stop for a chat, as he had to be up very early next morning. Uncle was disappointed, but we promised to go again soon. When we did go he had someone staying with him for six weeks, so there was no chance for our usual chat.

John fetched water from the river for the first time in July. Haymaking was going ahead, but the weather became very unsettled as usual, so it was late August before we finished. We were pleased to get 1,500 bales this year.

During the school holidays Michael and his friend Philip decided to cycle from Nailsea to Withypool with their tent. Some journey! They had one fine day before the rain started, first with squally showers and later with heavy, continuous rain. The camping field was very wet; the river covered the stepping-stones and beaches. Eventually the water was under their tent and the gales were lifting the pegs out. John decided to rescue them, so brought them back to Kinnings to dry out before returning home the next day. We took them as far as Taunton to minimise their journey.

David's father had been very poorly lately. David took him to a Nursing Home in Woolacombe, feeling he could get more attention there. Just two weeks later David was sent for, but by the time he arrived his father had died. We both went to his funeral at Barnstaple Crematorium. It was so sad for David, losing both parents within a year.

Betsy calved in September; a nice Charolais X heifer, but she gave me a nasty shock. We knew the calving was imminent so I had instructions to keep checking on her as John was off milk recording. I went down to Meadow at six fifty and found her completely stuck in the deep ditch with her calf behind her, almost hidden under branches and foliage. I rushed back to the house to ring

Sam and David. Sam and Christopher were quickly on the scene and managed to get them both out by the time David arrived from Presbury. Fortunately there were no ill effects to cow or calf. John missed that excitement!

One morning in October we found nine lambs in Lane Field and thought someone had probably put them in from the road. Next day we put them in Meadow for safety, waiting for someone to claim them. Another day passed. Then David rang and mentioned he had lost nine store lambs, so it was a relief to him, and to us, when he came and collected them. We were selling our sheep equipment at this time, as we had no intention of keeping them again.

The family were busy helping us in early November. Michael was helping John at David's. When the work was over they picked the last of David's Bramley apples for Maggie to take home, and also some swedes from his fields. Catherine was putting Presomet on the roof of the pigsties. She worked very hard until she ran out of Presomet, so John had to finish it off later. While they were here Kerry calved – a Hereford X Friesian heifer calf, which we decided to keep.

We had a great surprise on the evening of 9th November when we visited Uncle Ken. As soon as we sat down he went to his desk and produced a copy of Aunty Dolly's will. 'I want you both to read this,' he said. As expected all her money and possessions were willed to her husband, if he survived her. Otherwise it was left to John, including South Hill Farm and forty acres. We couldn't take it in. We were speechless. 'My will is exactly the same,' he told us.

There was a man, unrelated, who had lived with them for some years before his marriage who was expected to inherit. 'Why not him?' I asked.

'Because he has had enough from me. He doesn't need any more,' he replied rather sharply. He continued by saying how much he would like us to go and live with him. He was upset at the way his farm was deteriorating and wanted to see it being looked after again. It was such a surprise that we couldn't say yes straight away. He showed his disappointment, but assured us he would understand if we wanted to stay at Kinnings and the will would stand whatever we decided.

We spent an agonising two days debating the pros and cons. We loved Exmoor and South Hill and were very fond of Uncle Ken, yet we were so happy and doing so well at Kinnings. We had worked hard to improve it and had made good friends in the fourteen years we had lived there. It was a temptation to stay. Then we thought of Kenny, aged eighty-seven, in very poor health and living alone. There was really no choice. I wrote a long letter to him, saying we would be happy to come with him and how much we appreciated all he was doing for us.

We spent a whole day at South Hill on 23rd November and felt much happier about farming there. We promised Uncle we would put Kinnings up for sale in the spring. Throughout December we spent a considerable time sprucing up the outbuildings and clearing out rubbish. Our news had surprised our neighbours and friends, and still surprised us!

Chapter XVI

1986

This was the beginning of an exciting yet anxious year. We were committed to selling Kinnings in the spring and moving to Withypool, yet we still had to continue buying calves and farming as usual. We also had to make the place as presentable as possible before putting it on the market.

Our lane had been levelled at the end of December. In January John borrowed David's heavy roller and rolled it several times in readiness for quarry screenings. Fifty tons were delivered during the next few days, which John had to spread as soon as they arrived. It was dreadful weather for one load; heavy rain, hail and strong gales. Finally, several more rollings and the results were very worthwhile.

In the house I made 58 lbs of marmalade from Seville oranges, enough to last the next twelve months. On a dry day I picked several pounds of sprouts and prepared them for the freezer. John was sawing up plenty of wood for the fires or hedging. We were sending our four-month-old stirks (weaned calves) to market, two of them each week, and were getting about £230 each for them.

Uncle Ken came to dinner one day. He was very interested in our calves and suggested we bought some later on, started rearing them and then took them to South Hill when we moved across. He had a tenant on his forty acres, but it was agreed that he would leave in

September. Until then the calves would be housed in the shippen. We explained the situation to John May, a friendly dealer who had been buying calves for us for some years. He promised to look out for some good Charolais and Limousin bulls for us.

During February and March we were busy with paint and creosote, cleaning windows, washing curtains and cushion covers, and clearing out and burning rubbish. The recent gales had cracked some of the windows in the greenhouse and we replaced these, claiming insurance money from the NFU. We sold six weaned heifers at an average price of £145 each. We bought six Hereford X Friesian bull calves, also five Charolais X and five Limousin X bulls. We still managed to make visits to Withypool and one visit to Aunty Edie in Weymouth. It was an exhausting time.

In April we were ready to arrange for the sale of Kinnings. An auction sale was suggested but, as the reserved prices had not been reached on two recent farm auctions, we decided against it. The same day that the 'For Sale' notice was placed at our entrance we had a prospective buyer! It was the lady who the previous year had bought the land adjoining Kinnings, so it suited her perfectly. In just two weeks contracts were exchanged and completion date settled for 1st July.

Uncle Ken had been complaining of stomach pains for several months and they were becoming more severe. He said he would feel better when we moved in with him. Unfortunately, someone kept upsetting him by saying he was making a mistake in having us there, and this unpleasantness caused him considerable stress in addition to the pain.

Worse was to come when a couple of weeks later we had a message to say Uncle had fallen downstairs and been taken to East Reach hospital in Taunton. It seemed that we were getting the blame for this! It meant us having to move across to South Hill and sleep there, with John going home after early breakfast to attend to our animals. I stayed at South Hill to see to the campers. They were turning up in considerable numbers, as it was the Bank Holiday weekend at the end of May. Even our family turned up in their motorvan! We went to the hospital and discovered Uncle had been bringing an old carpet down the stairs when he tripped and fell. He was so apologetic about causing us trouble! Poor man, much of his body was black and blue with bruises.

Iain took Maggie and me to visit Uncle two days later. There was a little improvement and he was allowed home the next day. John fetched him, but we found him far from well. He was sick and felt very poorly and needed to stay in bed. A week later he felt a little better but was still unsteady on his legs, yet his doctor was quite pleased with him. Now the friend who had earlier stayed with him for six weeks returned, so John and I were able to go back to Kinnings.

John's first job was to cut the grass in Hill Field ready for haymaking. The weather had been dry for some time, but of course it rained for two days once we started. Fortunately it soon became hot and sunny again and we made 420 bales of good June hay, some of which was taken straight to Withypool.

On 17th June the auctioneers arrived to number all the lots for the next day's farm sale. We had a hectic time getting everything ready for the big day. It was heartbreaking having to let our furniture go, especially those items I had inherited from my mother that were connected with so many memories. However, there was no room for it at South Hill and Uncle had assured us that we could now consider everything there to be ours. We did find room for a couple of our single beds, small chairs and the microwave and freezer.

We were fortunate in having a warm, sunny day for the sale. Hill Field was perfect for car parking and Lane Field for setting out the implements and machinery. The cows were tied up in the shippen and all the calves in the cubicle house. The refreshment van arrived in good time, parked near the front garden and was soon doing a brisk trade. Bess put on a good 'I'm starving' act and came in for a few titbits!

The house effects were set out in the dining and top room, and when the people arrived there was hardly room to breathe. In addition to the furniture, there were books, china and glass, gramophone records, a cheese press and butter churn, a freezer, and our pretty French piano. The prices fetched were rather disappointing, probably because there were two larger sales in the area that same morning. However, this was more than compensated for by the excellent prices the cattle and implements made. Buyers were trying to persuade us to sell the exotic stirks, but these were promised for Withypool so we refused.

I was anxious about Lulu, our very special cow, who was now an eighth calver. She had calved recently, her bull calf fetching £212 at South Molton. The dealer who bought it mentioned this at our sale! I needn't have worried as Sam's brother-in-law, Ken Moore, bought Lulu, so I knew she would be well looked after.

Next morning when I looked into our top room and saw it empty I wept bitterly. What we were about to do had only just sunk in, but we were too busy to dwell on it.

We went to South Hill and put a new carpet in Uncle's bedroom. We cleaned out his shippen ready for the stirks as well as his calf houses at the back. John and David took two loads of hay across and then took the ten stirks. Uncle was upset that they couldn't go in the fields until September, when the tenant moved out, especially as the fields were often empty of stock.

On 25th June we said goodbye to Rosalyn and Sam and Mr and Mrs Wright. Mr Wright hugged me; he was so sorry to see us leaving. Next day we met Michael off the coach in South Molton. He had arrived to help us move to Withypool on the 27th. It was hard to leave Kinnings where we had been so happy, experiencing the greatest adventure of our lives.

At last we had arrived at South Hill, with Uncle Ken waiting in the garden, smiling and giving us a warm welcome. As I kissed him and gave him a hug, I thought if we could just make him happy it would be worth the sacrifice.

And so began a very different adventure, on beautiful Exmoor. But that is another story…

Printed in the United Kingdom
by Lightning Source UK Ltd.
101492UKS00001B/110